Alchemy

of

Healing

*Healing Relationship Endings from
Heartbreak into Wholeness
Inside the Alchemy of Nature*

LAURA ANNAN

One Vision Publishing

Alchemy of Healing
Healing Relationship Endings from Heartbreak into Wholeness
Inside the Alchemy of Nature
Copyright 2012 by Laura Annan

ISBN: 978-1-942338-98-7 (Print)
ISBN: 978-1-942338-93-2 (eBook)
One Vision Publishing
Published 2017

Photographs copyright © by Laura Annan
Cover Design: Laura Annan
Editor: Karren Tolliver

Subject: divorce care; divorce healing; self-help

~~~⚭~~~

Thank you for buying Alchemy of Healing.

CONTENTS

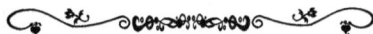

*"Never does Nature say one thing
and wisdom another."*
~ Juvenal

Why I Wrote This Book

For every ending, there is a new beginning.

LIFE IS A JOURNEY filled with various experiences that have the power to change the direction of our lives. How we navigate through the labyrinth of change, is how we consciously engage with life. There will always be goodbyes along the way. And after the ending of a relationship, a new beginning is waiting when we accept the invitation to heal our hearts.

When I first set out to start over after the ending of my 25-year marriage, I thought I could just move on and my life would naturally fall into place. However, life had other plans. The truth was—my heart was truly broken. I didn't recognize who I was anymore, or if I could ever love again.

Trying to rebuild my life led me to the majestic mountains of East Tennessee; not knowing I would embark on a healing journey. This special place is where Nature inspired me to find my way back to wholeness and changed my relationship with life.

I know firsthand there is no better place to heal and spiritually grow than being in the natural world. Why? The moment we step out into Nature, we are instantly surrounded by a creative force bigger than ourselves. Through her seasonal timing, she reveals that death, transformation, renewal and growth are parts of a constant cycle of change and movement. Reminding us that life is always in motion, and nothing stays the same.

By spending time in Nature, I began to understand how life also flows with the energy of movement that is necessary for our own personal growth. Being in Nature was nothing less than good healing medicine for my wounded heart and spirit. To work with that truth is a tremendous gift. I've been grateful every day since.

This book was birthed out of my healing journey to share with others. In the following chapters, we will turn to Nature as a source of inspiration to navigate the way. As your guide, I share nine stepping stones and offer transformational tools as the alchemy of healing heartbreak into wholeness. Upon completing this journey, you will experience wholeness to love freely once again.

Healing is a deep inner journey and is not an easy path to walk. Taking that first step into uncharted territory can be overwhelming when you don't have a map or guide to lead the way.

Why should you trust me as your guide? I understand how hard it is to start over when love still resides in the heart. I struggled with this life changing experience as much as I was transformed by it. What we share in common is heartbreak, while standing at a crossroads of a relationship ending.

If you are ready to embark on a transformational journey, I now invite you to take a breath and put one foot in front of the other to heal into wholeness—one stepping stone at a time. The only requirement needed is a willingness to bring all of yourself. Your healing path is your own, if you are ready to receive it.

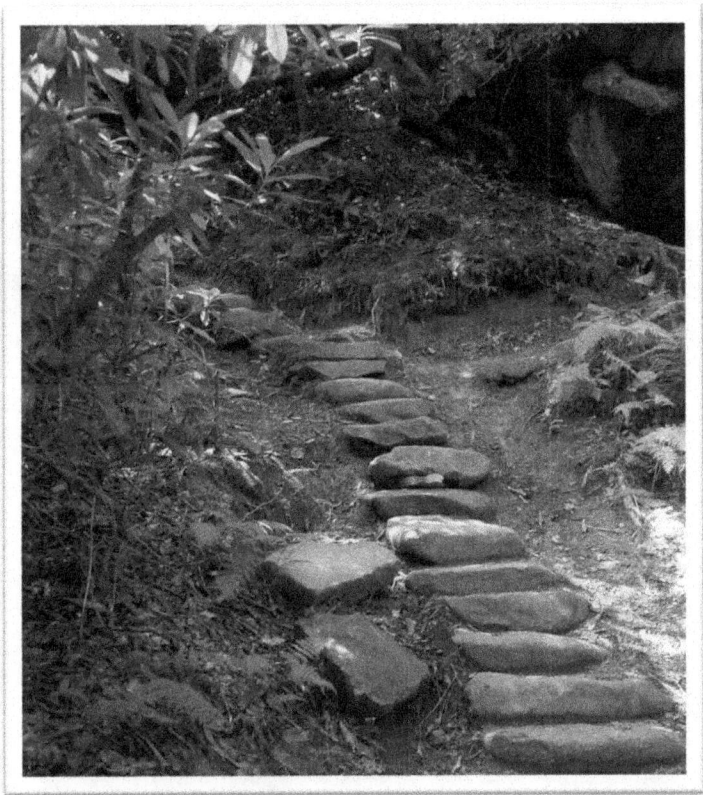

Stepping Stones

CROSSROADS

JOURNEY INTO THE UNKNOWN

*"I go to nature to be soothed and healed,
and to have my senses put in order."*

John Burroughs

My Journey Begins

---

*The bond of one is now torn apart leaving
behind a gaping emotional wound.*

THE FIRST STEP on my healing journey took place in the beautiful Great Smoky Mountains. Looking back, I'm not sure if I found this place or if it found me. Either way, hearing the *invitation* I could not refuse and took a leap into the unknown.

Being in Nature I discovered a great source of strength within myself, which encouraged the transformation necessary to heal my broken heart and cultivated a new loving relationship with myself during this difficult time. The more I nurtured this relationship, the more I was being pulled forward into a realm of awareness that comes from self-exploration.

Before guiding you on a healing journey, I must share my story that left me standing at a crossroads of heartbreak.

Breakup

I fell in love with a wonderful man. We rode into the sunset, built a life together and were growing old together—or so I thought. Twenty-five years later, the "happily ever after" simply became "after." Although we loved each other, our marriage had become a constant struggle that had outlived its time. The more we tried to fix it, the more we struggled and the further we grew apart. For many years it no longer

3

felt good to be in this relationship, but I held onto it because I was afraid to let go. I was afraid to accept my marriage was over.

My relationship ending came one day when everything imploded (in a destructive way) over something I don't even remember. That fateful day left us both to face the truth: we had stopped making each other happy, and we were no longer growing together as a couple. This didn't just happen overnight, it was festering for a long time. That moment was bittersweet.

Looking back now I understand it happened for a reason— our time together was over. After many years of struggling, it was time to move on with our lives without each other to find happiness once again. When you cannot do for yourself what needs to be done, the universe will intervene in a way that can no longer be denied–even if it's painful.

Not only did my marriage end but the business I co-owned, leaving me with no financial support. My life was crumbling around me. At the age of 48, I was left standing at the crossroads of my old life and a new life I could not yet imagine.

Although we parted on friendly terms, saying goodbye and starting over was to become the hardest undertaking I've ever experienced. With a heavy heart, I packed my car and headed to the mountains of East Tennessee. I had no idea what was ahead on this unknown road or why I was called to go there. It was a total leap of faith and had everything to do with wanting something more than being afraid of not doing it.

At that time, I wasn't sure if I was running from my old life or running to my new life. Somehow moving to a new state with no family, no friends and no job felt right. Sometimes you just have to start over to find yourself. And that's exactly what I did.

Breakdown

Even though ending my marriage was fated, it didn't soften the impact of how I was feeling. There was a heaviness in my heart.

I kept telling myself, *this too shall pass*. Yet it was becoming increasingly difficult to hide from the emotional impact when an unexpected surge of emotions knocked me to my knees. All the feelings I was avoiding came welling up like a violent storm.

A day didn't go by I wasn't haunted by the past or didn't play out old hurts left unhealed from the marriage. Asking myself repeatedly, *where did we go wrong?* I wondered what to do with the memories tormenting me. I questioned what happened to the love we once shared. W*here does the love go?* I was shattered and in the midst of those broken pieces, I asked myself, *where am I? Who am I?* My heart was broken, my spirit was broken . . . I was broken wide open.

I ached in places I didn't know one could ache as my emotions consumed me like a tidal wave taking my breath away. There was no escape from the sleepless nights of listening to the voices in my head berating me and playing out old scenarios, going over every detail of who said what and who did what, as I lay awake trying to fix what was impossible to fix.

There was nowhere to hide from all the emotions I was avoiding: sadness, anger, resentment. And with each passing day, more emotions showed up. Slowly I was spiraling into an abyss of despair, riddled with feelings of blame, shame and—most of all—failure.

I realized my emotions followed me to this new place of possibilities. Denying them was no longer an option. I didn't know what to do or who to turn to for help. Then, one night, while lying in bed, I prayed, *please help me find my way.*

Breakthrough

It always seems when you ask for help, the universe will conspire to support you by sending a message and a sign appears. That night in a dream, I was tumbling out of the sky when an angel caught me. "Everything is as it should be," the angel told me. "You have nothing to fear. It's time to return to Nature." I wept as she cradled me within her wings of protection. The dream abruptly ended and my angel vanished with it when the alarm clock sounded.

My dream world has always been an important part of my life that I listen to closely for guidance. Determined to understand the message I received, the angel's words echoed in my mind all day long.

Later that day while driving, I observed the beautiful views of the Smoky Mountains out in the distance. Being surrounded by the majestic mountains made me feel alive. When I moved here I looked forward to hiking, yet wallowing in self-pity was easier. Maybe I was punishing myself.

Laura, look at those beautiful mountains surrounding you, I told myself. *It's right there in front of you. What are you waiting for?* In that moment, inspiration hit. It was time to put on my hiking shoes and take a long overdue walk in the woods. *Maybe that's what the dream was trying to tell me.*

I tried hiking with groups and always found myself left behind in the rear, rather than "bagging" the trail, as so many of the hikers called it. I was much more interested in enjoying my surroundings than logging the miles. Ultimately, I ventured out on my own and started a hiking group called Women Walking in Nature. Organizing hikes to explore different waterfalls was one of the best times in my life and I made some lasting friendships.

Healing is a Personal Journey

During my time spent out in Nature, I experienced many magical and sometimes unexplainable moments. I could feel the movement of her primordial energy expanding within me as I set out on a path of self-healing. Her vibrational energy opened my heart, helping me to move beyond the emotional pain I was stuck in.

As I applied the observations witnessed in Nature, my pain was being lifted and my self-awareness shifted to look deeply within myself to find my own happily ever after. Small steps led to a major transformation, and over time my life fell into place with the tools I share in this book.

In many ways, my healing journey became a process of self-discovery and self-exploration, which allowed me to expand and enrich every area of my life.

I know it's easy to become lost in the gap between ending a relationship and beginning a new life, free from the emotional baggage. I also know that it's impossible to move forward when you're still holding love in your heart and holding onto what once was.

This healing journey starts where you are now—at the crossroads between endings and new beginnings. It begins with a single step into the unknown. Let's take that first step together.

Journey into the Unknown

*Whether the path in front of you
is lit or hidden, trust that your feet
will always land firmly on the ground.*

ALTHOUGH RELATIONSHIPS MAY be divinely ordained, not all relationships last forever. When the relationship time is over, it leaves a hollowness that echoes with emotional hurt and uncertainty. It can feel like your heart is literally broken.

Relationships are part of our greatest learning experiences, but the hardest relationship we will ever have to face is the one we have with ourselves when we're standing at a crossroads, left broken wide open where the road of love has ended.

But what if relationship endings are an *invitation* to explore life a little more?

Even though going through the ending of a relationship can be a soul-crushing experience, it also has the ability to open you up to another powerful growth experience. Now, life is offering the next *experience* to be explored and wants to be lived through you. This means meeting the fullness of life where you are and moving through it.

Endings are an invitation to embark on a healing journey for growth and transformation to take back your life.

Standing at a Crossroads

Standing at a crossroads, we think of a fork in the road forming a "Y" which says it all–*why*. Why am I standing here? Why did this happen to me?

When we meet someone and fall in love, it's because we are open to receive it and we easily move into a cycle of new life experiences to explore. But, it doesn't mean it's our life plan. Not all love stories stand the test of time when fate brings us to a crossroads, a parting of ways–an unexpected fork in the road–where what once was familiar now becomes the unknown.

And when the relationship ends, it now leaves us open, once again, to move into another cycle of new life experiences to explore. This new cycle of change is not always easy to transition into because it's not as joyful as falling in love. This life experience can be very painful.

Nevertheless, we can assure ourselves this *ending* has come our way because we are meant to experience it, to feel it, and to grow from it. A time to explore our emotions and heal the split within, to be fully liberated from the past. It all starts while standing at the crossroads of the past and the future.

This crossroads of the life you knew and the unknown life that lies ahead is where the healing journey begins. Even though you may feel as though your life has fallen apart, perhaps even powerless to move forward, the journey of life always marches on. It's important to understand life will continue in a different way.

Answering the *invitation* that is calling to you now is a life experience that will deepen your spiritual growth. Because you are a spiritual being, every experience paves the way for growth to emerge at a deep evolutionary level. All experiences are valuable–even heartbreak.

This journey you are about to embark upon will at times be lonely, painful and difficult. It will no doubt have many twists and turns where powerful obstacles may seek to block your way. Yet, what's uncovered within the journey is a healing path in discovering yourself a little more for wholeness to emerge.

Cultivating your own power to save yourself is at the very heart of the invitation because the truth is—no one else can do this for you.

Healing is an Inner Journey

Your capacity to make sense of what is happening varies. You may easily become overwhelmed with emotions and thoughts of *should of, could of, would of,* causing a destructive inner struggle that may close off your heart or even develop into illness if you remain in denial for long enough. Whatever feelings you are experiencing at this time are not to be judged, dismissed, or denied. Instead, acknowledge, embrace and honor them so you can move through them to receive healing.

To succeed on the journey is to trust the process of life fated especially for you to experience. This requires a willingness to be vulnerable so you can confront any hidden, unpleasant, or unspoken emotions you may be holding on to. If you instead avoid those emotions, you are only handing over your power to them and now they own you in an unhealthy way.

Your own emotional pain is the only thing holding you hostage and your healing journey is not complete until you heal the pain for yourself. No friend, no relative and no new relationship can do that for you. The journey is complete when your emotional pain no longer holds you captive.

Step by step, this healing journey holds the potential to change the quality of your life. The more you cultivate your ability to move forward in life, the more you will easily move into change with grace. And you will begin to trust that life is happening *for* you instead of *to* you.

Looking back is the familiar path of where you've already been. Looking ahead is the unknown path leading the way to new discoveries meant for you to explore. Not knowing what lies ahead is a natural part of life. The unknown path is the only way out. If you accept the *invitation*, it means you are ready to heal your heartbreak.

Before embarking on a journey into healing, we must understand life is a perfectly orchestrated system of forward movement. Learning Nature's patterns of movement helps us to make sense of our own internal emotional landscape when navigating transitions in life.

Even in the midst of what appears to be chaos, there is a natural order always moving towards growth. Within Nature is the alchemy of transformation through movement.

Alchemy Inside Nature

Nature is always talking to us,
opening a window to our spirit
and inspiring our heart.

ANCIENT WISDOM TEACHES us, in the beginning, there was the universe that gave way to the creation of unity through the natural elements of earth, air, fire, water and spirit. Unity is our relationship with ourselves, our relationship with others and our relationship with the natural elements themselves, as we learn to live in harmony with life, rather than struggling against it.

This sacred relationship of unity reminds us that we are deeply connected to the energetic flow of Nature because we evolved within the movement of the natural world. We are all children of the earth, we belong to the earth and the earth is a part of us. This interconnectedness with Nature is deeply imprinted in our spiritual DNA—it's a place called home.

Nature is everywhere because she is the original healer. She is everything because the natural world provides us with good healing medicine for our mind, our body and our spirit. Nature reveals a universal compass by which to navigate life. By reconnecting with her creative energies we can honor the movement of life necessary for our own personal growth.

Inside Nature, there is a language of creative energies naturally taking place. Everything is alive. Everything is energy and according to science, energy cannot be destroyed—it only changes form and is always in motion.

Alchemy of Healing

Alchemy is the fundamental element of changing matter into form. When change happens, the old form falls away, and a new form takes place to continue the natural flow of movement. Movement activates the co-creative forces of alchemy in the natural world.

Nature speaks to us in many ways through her patterns of movements within the seasonal landscape where transition is the common energetic thread. As winter awakens from the slumber of regeneration, it gives way for the renewal of spring to be birthed. Then summer moves in to celebrate growth until it's time to retreat into autumn, where the pattern of movement completes the growing cycle and turns to winter once again. This never-ending circle of movement is a constant flow of change; sometimes gentle and gradual while at other times violent and destructive.

Change, then, is a vital part of Nature, whose seasonal timings are nothing more than energy changing form teaching us that death, regeneration, transformation and growth make up the rhythm of life. This movement of change is a creative part of the natural world, just as change is part of the human experience because, similarly, life also flows by the energy of movement. Understanding there is a natural progression of movement where the landscape changes and the mood changes can help us to understand and experience change as the movement of life.

Movement is the alchemy reinforcing our unity of living in harmony with life. Life is a journey, with many different experiences to explore along the way. We are here to grow from each experience that is presented.

Journey into the Unknown

Matters of the heart are the most challenging when it comes to navigating through heartbreak since the connection we have to the past and to others creates heartfelt strings of attachment. When the relationship time is over, separation can be painful.

Being able to move through our experiences, even when it's unpleasant, is an important component of how we consciously grow and evolve with life. Healing pain brings the greatest reward–to live life lighter.

This healing journey, you are about to embark upon, is a path of inner transformation helping you to navigate one stepping stone at a time from heartbreak into wholeness.

Navigating the Journey

A healing journey is essentially a spiritual exercise of exploring our inner world.

WHERE THERE IS heartbreak, there is love. Love never dies; it just changes form. And just as your journey with your former partner began with love, this healing journey back to wholeness will also end with love when you invest the time and energy to heal yourself.

It's been said time heals all wounds and on some level it's true, but you need to take *action* to *move through* healing. Waiting for time to tick away is not the antidote. Movement changes the energy of time, paving a way to wholeness.

To succeed on this journey is to take action, as each stepping stone requires movement. With each step the transformation you experience will help carry you to the next step where you will gain insights about how your thoughts and actions influence the choices you make; including the choice to either live in the past or to move forward.

It's important to know your healing journey will be unique because it will reveal the emotional pain you are holding onto. This inward and intimate experience will push you to feel into yourself and to be vulnerable. This, in itself, is an act of self-perseverance, which is necessary to navigate through what lies ahead.

How far you travel on the journey is up to you if you're willing to do the inner healing work required. By doing the inner work, you are building a relationship with yourself that is the key to creating inner peace and harmony to put the past where it belongs—behind you—to love freely again.

As we travel on the journey, we have travel companions helping us with nurturing ways to connect more deeply with our heart and spirit to navigate the way. Let's explore the transformational tools we'll discover through each of the stepping stones.

INNER COACH AFFIRMATIONS

Affirmations replace critical self-talk with empowering messages.

Neuroscientists say it's not unusual to think more than 50,000 thoughts a day. Most of those thoughts aren't particularly helpful, especially the critical self-talk messages. When we accept these critical statements as the truth, they hold great power over the kind of life we create for ourselves.

During my healing journey, I turned to affirmations suggested by Louise L. Hay in her book, *You Can Heal Your Life*. I originally bought the book back in 1998 when I was going through a difficult time, but I put it down because I wasn't ready to do the inner work that was necessary. After my belongings arrived at my new home, the only thing I was excited about was finding my books. Opening the first box, right on top was the book I had put down a decade ago. Interesting how it showed up, when I needed it the most. In that moment, I was finally ready to do the inner work.

Every day I would read a section, and recite affirmations. In a short amount of time, I started to find inner peace as the affirmations began to lead my life in a new direction. The affirmations became the fuel I needed to move into a new state of awareness with a new perspective about my situation. After my healing journey, I attended a Hay House

"I Can Do It" weekend where I was inspired to become a certified Heal Your Life Teacher® and later began leading group workshops. This much I know for sure—affirmations work and they have the power to change your life.

Our thoughts are a powerful source of creation and manifestation–they can lift us up or tear us down. We all have the capability to change our critical self-talk and redirect our thinking with encouraging statements of affirmations. Think of affirmations as your inner coach for positive empowered thinking always available for you to use.

How to use the affirmations presented here:

1. Write each affirmation on an index card and carry it with you until you memorize it.

2. Post the cards as a reminder around the house, in your car, or at work.

3. Schedule a daily reminder each day. When the reminder goes off, stop, close your eyes and mentally recite the affirmation three times.

Repetition works well to quiet the critical self-talk in our head, so feel free to recite (or even sing) the affirmations daily. Saying affirmations silently works great, but standing in front of a mirror and saying the affirmation out loud is even more powerful. Try it and see for yourself!

Call up your inner coach affirmations every time the self-defeating chatter distracts you from progressing on your path.

EXPLORATION JOURNAL

Keeping an exploration journal is a great tool for deepening your sense of connection with what is going on around you and what is emerging within you.

Writing in a journal is one of the oldest methods of self-exploration. There are many studies about the benefits of journaling. Researchers found that 10-15 minutes of writing does wonders for managing the stress of our daily lives, and it's also an effective way to reflect on the moments of your day.

Benefits of Journaling:

- Clears out the self-talk buzzing in your head.
- Writing down how you feel is immensely liberating.
- What surfaces and reveals itself is often cathartic.

Journaling is a valuable way to gain self-awareness. Writing about thoughts and feelings not only helps to process them, it also helps to clear out any thoughts you are stuck obsessing over. Allowing restless thoughts to come alive on the pages helps to release them. Once the words are written, somehow—as if by magic—the energy changes.

To get started, I encourage you to find a beautiful notebook or a journal. Find a quiet place to record your thoughts. Free write for 5-10 minutes about whatever you're feeling or thinking. With no judgment, let it all out on the pages. As you write, keep the pen moving by allowing the words to flow with no editing. Be open and honest. You may discover truths you didn't know existed until the words hit the page.

On the healing journey the more you journal, the greater insights you will gain about who you are. Exploration is a step towards obtaining self-awareness of your life. As a daily practice, here are some starting prompts when you're staring at a blank page:

- Right now, I am feeling...
- Three things I learned about myself today are...
- Five things I am thankful for today are...

A journal is also a great way to build a book of "you" by filling up the pages with inspiring pictures, cards, meaningful quotes, or anything that speaks to you. Decorate the pages. Draw in it. Write poems. There's no right or wrong way to keep a journal. Have fun with it!

INSIDE THE ALCHEMY OF NATURE

Nature is essentially the original healer; she can heal our wounds, water our hearts and restore our lives.

Our ancestors lived in harmony with the natural elements, as they were attuned to the growing cycles of Nature. Their bond with the natural world influenced every aspect of life.

It's no secret that the earth is a living and breathing, creative vibration with organic healing powers always available to us. By simply being outside in Nature, we can unite with the elemental forces of air, water, earth and fire to absorb the healing energies they provide. Developing a relationship with the natural world helps to live in greater harmony with the creation of our own life.

I know firsthand there is no better place to heal and grow than in Nature, not only to mend the emotional wounds of life but also to help find balance whenever we need it. Spending time in Nature is a type of therapy that nourishes us with a restorative energy providing good medicine for our mind, body and has the power to intoxicate our spirit.

Whenever possible, get out in Nature where you can feel the natural pace of the earth and start to slow down from the hyperactive pace of our modern world. The more time you spend outside, the more you connect with life on a deeper level by accessing the essential life-giving elements through the alchemy of Nature therapy.

With all journeys, there is a beginning. To heal heartbreak is to step through it. Are you ready? Let's take that first step and set the intention of commitment.

Whenever possible, get out in Nature where you can feel the natural grace of the earth and start to slow down from the hyperactive pace of our modern world. The more time you spend outside, the more you connect with life on a deeper level and access the essential life-giving elements through the ancient power of Nature therapy.

With all journeys, there's a beginning. To heal heartbreak is to stop the spiral. Are you ready? Let's take that first step toward the intention of commitment.

Stepping Stone 1

COMMITMENT

THE FIRST STEP on any healing journey begins by activating a *commitment* to yourself. Your healing must be attended to and knowing you are the one directly influencing your healing is the key in turning heartbreak around.

A *commitment* grows from a willingness to listen deeply to your own needs. This willingness is an act of self-care, which is necessary to build a deeper relationship with YOU. Building this relationship supports you along the journey.

Think of your healing journey as sacred and honor every step along the way. Although you may suffer some setbacks along the way, don't beat yourself up over it. Just as the dawning of a new sunrise, every day brings a new opportunity to start again—so be gentle and compassionate with yourself. Now, more than ever, is the time to be extra loving and patient with yourself.

Commitments to ourselves are the ones we tend to find most challenging, and yet they have the most potential to make the greatest difference in our lives.

Time to Heal

Pain arises from loving someone who is no longer in our life. When we take the time to honor the healing process, then we are no longer walking against it—we are walking alongside it to be fully present with it. Allow yourself time to heal.

Everything that happens to us; happens to us in and through time. Time is the force opening us to new experiences to explore. There's no need to rush through the journey. A year in time is a natural cycle, as Nature illustrates, to move full circle through the healing process. Why a year?

Like the seasons themselves, the cycle of a year in time activates your own healing power to release all the emotional debris you are holding. A cycle of time to reconnect back to yourself, and to prepare your heart for a new experience of love.

Just think how much you can grow in a year.

In Solitude

Healing begins when you take the time to be with yourself. Understanding who you are now, after the relationship, is the most important self-caring act you can do for yourself. By doing so, healing will bring a completion for wholeness to fully emerge.

While you are healing is not the time to be in a relationship. It's easy to believe the only way to get over a relationship ending is by getting under another relationship right away. A new relationship will not heal the broken parts of you. It's time to focus on yourself now and it's THE most important thing you can do to heal completely before getting into another relationship.

Give up any illusion that jumping into a new relationship will either make you feel better or will help you to move on. If the emotional wounds from your previous relationship remain unhealed, they will unintentionally be carried into a new relationship.

Relationships are sacred unions of emotional and physical bonding that are immensely intertwined. A spiritual connection takes place when we fall in love with someone, and this person becomes a part of us. Even though you are physically separated from your former partner, the connection is still present. Part of the journey is to release the emotional connection before you can freely love again.

When you no longer have feelings of attachment to your former partner or strong emotional reactions about your former partner, and when you no long fear what *could* happen in a new relationship, then you are ready to meet a new person without sabotaging the relationship with old unhealed wounds.

Filling the Void

Starting a new relationship would be filling a "we" void. Do not fear the void. Instead, it's best to embrace the void and fill the void by spending time alone. Yes, this may be challenging, especially when society puts such an emphasis on being in a relationship but when you go deep into the void, you will find courting a new relationship with YOU will transform your life and satisfy the void.

The fear of being alone sends many running into the arms of another relationship too soon. Seeking a relationship to escape from loneliness is a dangerous road to travel. Don't rush into a new relationship out of loneliness because the only person you will attract now will not heal you into wholeness.

Often being alone with our thoughts and feelings is scarier than being physically alone. Being lonely may feel miserable at times but now is the time to heal from the effects of your relationship and tend to your inner world.

After healing, you can then safely enter into a new relationship with someone else. This also holds true should you decide, ultimately, to remain single. Being single should be a conscious, empowered decision and not one made from a place of being afraid to fall in love again, or by shutting down your heart to ensure what happened in your last relationship won't happen again.

You are already in the most important relationship you will ever have—the one with YOU! You were born into it and will live in it. Make it a good one!

The first stepping stone is a *commitment* to spend this healing time nurturing a loving relationship with yourself. It starts with an intention of being able to show up in your life in a supportive way.

Exploration Journal

Begin your journaling exploration on this stepping stone by giving yourself permission to support your healing. The best way to do this is by handwriting a letter of *commitment* to yourself.

Take out your journal and with pen in hand write yourself a heartfelt letter explaining why your healing is important to you. Let it flow. Resist the temptation to be perfect. No need to edit yourself. Let your heart be your guide.

When you are finished, read your letter out loud to yourself. Speaking the words you wrote, projects this *commitment* into the deepest reaches of your spirit, where your thoughts, feelings and behaviors line up and you experience an inner and outer cooperation which moves you forward to the first level of transformation on your journey.

It may be helpful to repeat this exercise for several days. This process of repetition allows you to get out of your head and into your heart. You will find writing the same thoughts over and over again will eventually open up a space where letting go happens naturally and self-defeating thoughts begin to fade away.

Realize your strength to stay on track may be tested daily. Make a sincere *commitment* every day and feel the miracle of healing happening.

Inner Coach Affirmation

I Am Committed

Words carry an energy. Affirmations are a great way to help you stay on track. Recite them throughout your day to yourself as you walk, drive to work, take a shower, brush your teeth, wait in line or at a stop light, when you first wake up, when you go to bed. Anytime!

COMMITMENT

I am
committed
to my
healing
journey

Journey into the Unknown

Alchemy Inside Nature

Nature Treatment

By observing and appreciating Nature, we are invited to experience ourselves in a new way. Being outside increases wellness, promotes creativity, and engages the senses.

Our fast-paced, high-tech world of electronic devices, demands and a drive to get more done, has left us living in two worlds of distractions. Our *outer* world is filled with multi-tasking, meeting deadlines, rushing around through our day and attending to social media, email and texts. Our *inner* world is just as busy, always wandering from one thought to another with a constant stream of chatter creating more demands and more problems to solve.

We basically think we're in control of both worlds. Yet they seem to control us, driving us in the direction it desires.

Both the demands of our outer world and inner world can ultimately lead to stress, anxiety, depression and even serious health problems. And more importantly, they disconnect us from living in the present moment which is why we need to unplug from the busyness to find a sense of inner peace of just *being* rather than always *doing*.

When we take time out to reconnect with the simple beauty of living in the moment, we begin to cultivate balance in our lives. How can we do this? By taking a walk!

The simple act of taking a walk increases well-being and deepens our connection to the present moment where life is really happening.

Spending time in Nature creates a sense of peace and harmony, alleviates stress, promotes creativity and engages the senses. A place where we can instantly destress and just *be*.

With that in mind, go take a walk in Nature. Walk through a local park; walk in your neighborhood; walk along a beach; walk in a garden; walk in a forest; walk anywhere.

As you do so, witness your surroundings and tune into the moment. Look up and explore the sky. Look around and be curious about what you see. Be the observer. Take everything in and consciously engage your senses to deepen your connection to your surroundings. Focus on the sights, sounds and smells around you. Feel how your body naturally begins to relax. Notice how your mind begins to settle down.

While walking, be mindful. Observe what you see and name it: *I see clouds floating in the sky. I feel a breeze against my skin. I smell the fragrance of flowers. I hear the sound of birds singing.*

When your mind starts to wander, simply refocus your attention back to the present moment and start observing all over again. This time, see if you notice something new.

Remember, this is *your* time—it's not the time to be talking on the phone or texting. You may find it challenging to avoid giving into the temptation of checking your messages or emails but resist it. You can attend to the social world when you're done walking. It will still be there.

ALCHEMY OF HEALING

- *Endings are an invitation to embark on a healing journey for growth and transformation to take back your life.*

- *Cultivating your own power to save yourself is at the very heart of the invitation because the truth is—no one else can do this for you.*

- *Affirmations replace critical self-talk with empowering messages.*

- *Keeping an exploration journal is a great tool for deepening your sense of connection with what is going on around you, and what is emerging within you.*

- *Nature is essentially the original healer; she can heal our wounds, water our hearts, and restore our lives.*

- *Commitments to ourselves are the ones we tend to find most challenging, and yet they have the most potential to make the greatest difference in our lives.*

As the earth moves through the seasons each year, so too do we move through the seasons of death, regeneration, transformation and growth opening an awareness to our relationship with our own lives. Understanding the alchemy of movement can help us to navigate through change to fully experience life as it is.

Nature teaches us there is a creative process: a natural flow, a natural movement. Change is a universal theme and affects the very nature of our experiences to explore. Our sacred journey of life is to retreat, regenerate, renew and reintegrate again and again when life is happening for us.

How we respond to the circumstances of our life has a direct impact on how we choose to live our life. We can resist life or we can move forward in life when we are willing to be with it for our spiritual growth.

Commitment is a stepping stone of taking the time to be attentive to our own healing. The road to healing is a journey of self-exploration to learn new ways of overcoming what we believe to be life's obstacles. This path leads the way towards stepping into wholeness.

Journey Notes

Being alone, at first, was very uncomfortable since I had been married for most of my adult life. Facing the fact I was no longer part of a "we," I set out on a journey to find "me." There hadn't been a "me" in a very long time and I wasn't even sure who that person was anymore.

During my time alone, I learned a partner cannot carry me in life. It's up to me to make my own life and find my own happiness. I kept telling myself: *Believe in yourself. You are a capable person with infinite potential!*

The deeper I explored Nature, the more I discovered how her movement of change also applies to the human experience. As a part of creation, we are governed by the same universal laws. Change is the only constant in life.

AUTUMN RETREATS

JOURNEY INTO LETTING GO

*"In every walk with nature one receives
far more than he seeks."*

John Muir

On The Trail

JAKES CREEK GAP

Trailhead: Jakes Creek Gap; GSMNP
Features: Quiet forest walk, streams, historical site
Rating: Easy
Distance: 4.6 roundtrip
Elevation: 1,909 ft.
Date: 9.25.08

Turning to face the clock, it read 6 a.m. Once again my day began with another sleepless night. My mind raced with endless thoughts, retelling stories from the past like an old broken record: *Why this? Why that?* Instead of turning over and trying to get some much needed rest, I obediently got out of bed and off I went for a walk in the woods.

35

The winding road through the town of Townsend, leading to the Great Smoky Mountains National Park, was covered with fog. As the sun made its grand appearance over the mountains, the mist slowly faded away. It was going to be a beautiful autumn day. Turning towards Elkmont campground, I couldn't wait to hit the trail!

With no trail map, I decided to follow the signs as my guide. Jakes Creek Gap Trailhead started out on an old gravel road then slowly began to twist and turn along the contours of Curry Mountain. Along the trail, old run-down cabins and stonewall rumbles were signs left behind from the once thriving community.

Autumn was in full swing! With each crunchy step, I witnessed the landscape exploding with vibrant colors of yellow, red, and orange. Birds were flying around the treetops. Chipmunks were chasing each other over logs. The cool wind swung the tree branches, shaking and tossing off the leaves. They swirled and twirled in the air before letting go, floating gracefully and landing gently to weave a calico carpet on the ground.

Walking and watching the leaves dancing in the crisp air was magical. I was enjoying every moment until the trail split into two separate paths. Looking around, there were no visible trail signs or markers to lead the way. Feelings of confusion began to bubble up inside of me. *Which way do I go?* I didn't want to get lost, but that's exactly how I felt as I was faced with my own reality. Falling to my knees, I fell apart. *How did I get to this place of feeling lost?*

Through my wet eyes, I witnessed the leaves falling in celebration, dancing with the wind. They naturally separated from the trees, surrendering to their fate as a symbolic sacrament of death and letting go for a new growing cycle.

On that autumn day, from the top of Curry Mountain, I was able to witness life from a different perspective with a new awareness. I was holding onto something that was no longer mine to hold onto.

Nature taught me the subtle dance of detachment, and inspired me to fully embrace my reality. It was time to accept my marriage was over and surrender to a new direction as a new growing cycle was beginning for me, too.

Journey Into Letting Go

Autumn retreats as a symbolic death,
where some part of you must die before
another part can emerge and come to life.

IN AUTUMN CHANGE begins to take place as Nature retreats from her yearlong journey around the growing cycle. The mood changes as day and night rendezvous on the Autumnal Equinox, parting ways in exchange for shorter days and longer nights.

The landscape transforms as Nature performs her seductive ritual of letting go. Within this blazing farewell, the natural landscape explodes with vibrant color as the leaves gradually begin to drop and gently drift earthward, where they will decompose and become nutrients for the soil.

Leaves accept they must let go and surrender to their fate. Imagine if a tree carried the same leaves year after year. At some point, the tree would not be able to support new growth and in time the branches would break from carrying such a heavy load. Eventually, the tree would wither away from holding onto something it can no longer support.

Letting go is the alchemy for something new to grow.

Inside the Alchemy of Autumn

In Nature letting go is effortless, yet as humans we tend to hold on tightly to the familiar because our thoughts, security, and our identity easily become attached to a relationship. The connection we have with someone is deeply rooted and often leads to deep sorrow pulling us beyond our comfort zone.

When we unite with the season of autumn, we begin to understand how the subtle dance of the changing landscape in our own lives can be supported by accepting what is and surrendering into every moment that is now presented.

Letting go is difficult because it's hard to understand endings as part of our evolutionary growth on the journey of life. But it's impossible to move forward if we are still holding onto something that no longer belongs to us.

Divorce is a death of a marriage, a death of a relationship and a death of a partnership. Letting go of someone we love, as painful as it may be, is the alchemy to *Acceptance* and *Surrender* as we navigate our way for healing to transpire through the next two stepping stones.

Stepping Stone 2

ACCEPTANCE

ONE OF THE hardest aspects of divorce and ending a relationship is saying goodbye to the person you love and saying goodbye to the familiar life you know.

Trying to move on when love still remains in the heart is a process. Letting go of love is not easy. This is a transitional time that feels like everything is falling apart, and we're not sure what to hold onto anymore. It certainly is a confusing time when relationship endings come our way.

Acceptance allows "what is" whether it's welcomed or not.

Holding On

Acceptance opens a space of taking responsibility for being completely honest with ourselves. Otherwise, we abandon the reality that life is *happening* for us. Trusting the process is no easy task, but no one can create a new beginning by clinging to the notion that life can be any different from what it is at this very moment.

Thinking about how to go back in time and fixing it only brings denial and deeper wounds to heal. Why hold yourself a prisoner of believing anything else? It's time to embrace the truth: the relationship time is over.

With *acceptance,* there is no "right" or "wrong." No finger pointing. No blame. There is never anything that needs to be fixed or changed. It is what it is.

To move one step closer into wholeness is to accept the truth as it is and to understand you are actually where you need to be on your journey of life. *Acceptance* is forward movement and saying *yes* to life.

Check in with yourself right now. Are you struggling to hold onto your relationship?

If you are, then without *acceptance* you will continue to struggle against the truth and stay in a perpetual state of resistance. Where there is resistance, there is attachment. Where there is attachment, there is no room for letting go.

Resistance

When the relationship time is over it's easy to be attached to your former partner, attached to the life you made together, attached to the comfort of where you've been. Deep attachment stems from the emotional connection we have with another person where the bond of another is woven tightly together with yours. Attachment weaves a tangled web of resistance.

When a relationship dies, a part of you dies along with it. You will have to mourn not only the death of a relationship but also your death as well since a piece of your life story has died along with the marriage. A natural response may be to resist on a physical, mental, or emotional level. By accepting the truth, you are facing life with more awareness.

If instead, you choose to resist the reality that your relationship is over and you continue to cling to the past, you are only pushing against reality. There is also the risk your relationship with other family members, especially as parents, now becomes challenged, which can create an unpleasant environment. This is not healthy for you or your family.

Resistance is not forward movement, and it comes at a price. The longer you resist, the harder it will be to hold onto something that is no longer yours. Trying to hold onto a relationship after it ends only prolongs the pain of heartbreak.

Nothing exists, except the reality that the relationship is over. Letting go of the relationship empowers your ability to consciously acknowledge that you are exactly where you are.

Start Where You Are

The only way to get somewhere is to first understand where you are. You are here in this moment, trying to heal your broken heart.

Please love yourself enough to let go of how you think your life should be right now. It may be hard to understand now but you will survive, you will heal your heart, and you will love again.

Acceptance is the alchemy that shifts the energy of movement. Now is the time to accept what is and start where you are to move forward into the next season of your life.

Inner Coach Affirmation

I ACCEPT WHERE I AM

There's a little voice in our head many call the "false-self" that wants to set up roadblocks to undermine our journey. It likes to tell us stories we begin to believe. This voice, this false-self, has something to say but is it telling the truth? It's best to let the voice speak without engaging and thank her for sharing. Then begin to quiet the voice by calling upon your inner coach.

ACCEPTANCE

I accept
where
I am
on the
journey
of life

Journey into Letting Go

Stepping Stone 3

SURRENDER

STEPPING INTO SURRENDER is an opportunity to trust in the process that life will unfold as it is meant to, without our intervention. Within this space is the freedom of liberating ourselves from the bondage of our own expectations and understanding we are not in control of all aspects of life.

Surrender can be a fear-based word because for many it means submission or weakness. As a culture, our tendency is to micro-manage and use our will power to control everything we can because the ego mind (false-self) feeds on the survival-based need to fight or flee. The false-self wants us to believe we can control situations, other people, and it convinces us we'll be successful in doing so.

Yet *surrender* can be appreciated as a great strength when we give up the resistance to control what we cannot know—how the outcome of any given situation will unfold. By leaning into *surrender*, we can work with whatever situation comes our way and learn from it.

Be open to allowing life to unfold with no need to chase after trying to fix things because the right moment to act and the right solution will always present itself when we put some distance between a situation without being reactive. Distance is always an advantage when we withdraw in order to regain our center. Patience is a valuable virtue for a solution to emerge.

Solutions Always Exist

We all get caught up in trying to control areas of our lives and being obsessed with outcomes. It's natural to want a situation to happen in our time and in the way we expect it to happen.

When we become fixated on a certain outcome, we start to think our way through it, imagining how it should happen. And when it doesn't happen exactly as we imagined, there's a tendency to force the outcome to be what it isn't capable of being.

Life doesn't always happen in the way we think or believe it should be. As long as we try to micro-manage the details, it's impossible to get in the flow of life.

Surrender is not a demand; it's not forcing life to go one way or the other. Rather, it's letting go into how life wants to be. Allowing circumstances to unfold organically paves the way with a knowing that everything will work out in the end for everyone involved.

If you're willing to let go of control and lean into *surrender* a new experience will emerge. The universe always has more compelling plans for us than we can ever imagine.

Surrender is a willingness to trust life is working its way through you and everything will work out for your highest good.

Shift the Energy

We cannot be fully in control of our lives and outside influences. We have no real power over people or our environment, despite our attempts. Trying to work out the details or forcing things will ultimately fail because control is unattainable. Control is only an illusion, one we chase after endlessly to our disadvantage.

With *surrender,* you can begin to accept the idea you are not in control of everything after all. It's best to take your hands off the wheel and allow life to take you where you need to go. Instead of forcing life, now you are in a constant flow of being connected with life while it is trying to move through you.

Often, we expect ourselves to recover quickly from divorce. When we don't, we may feel hopeless. The alchemy of *surrender* will clear the path of stepping through life with no looming false ideals.

Since you cannot control what your healing will look like, you can only focus on how you choose to explore the healing experience. It's important to remember, as you *surrender* in each moment, the more you grow towards allowing the organic movement of healing to unfold.

Inner Coach Affirmation

I AM WILLING TO LET GO

The only real power we have over our thoughts is when we *surrender* into becoming the observer of our thoughts. As the observer, we begin to realize we are not the thinker. This awareness activates a higher level of self-awareness.

SURRENDER

I Am
willing
to let go
of all
expectations

Journey into Letting Go

Exploration Journal

LETTING GO

In the midst of the healing journey, you may push against your experiences by trying to dictate how life should be. Resistance only creates more suffering.

Let's explore what you're holding onto in this next exercise. Be willing to be honest with yourself and resist the temptation to edit your thoughts. Let the words flow.

To begin, find a quiet place where there are no distractions. Before bringing pen to paper close your eyes and place your hand on your heart. This simple yet effective touch has the power to self-soothe. Placing your hand on your heart is a great way to connect with your body and helps to center you in the present moment.

Next, take some nice, deep, cleansing breaths. With each breath, allow your body to relax and release any tension it may be holding. If it feels comfortable for you, ask for guidance.

When you are ready, open your eyes and write down the first impression that comes to mind for each journal prompt listed below.

1. What thoughts am I still holding onto about my relationship?

   Example: We will get back together again if I give it some time.

> Usually, what we are holding onto is some type of expectation or fear. A fear we don't want to admit or don't even realize exists. Once you understand what's going on internally, you will be able to see what you need to let go of.

2. What areas of my life are being challenged at this time by feelings of worry, doubt and stress?

   Example: I worry that I will not find another relationship again. I am afraid to love again.

3. How can I *surrender* into these challenges to reduce my stress?

   Example: I *surrender* into my life; if it's meant to be, it will be.

When you are finished place your arms around yourself and give yourself a big hug. It takes courage to be honest with yourself. Be proud—one step leads to another.

Alchemy Inside Nature

TAKE A BREATH OF AIR

The greatest gift we can give ourselves is to spend more time out in the natural world. By stepping outside and breathing in Nature's creative energy we can lift our spirits and then approach life again, renewed.

Our breath is a vital life force, yet most of the time we're not aware of just how disconnected we can become from it. Our breath has the power to help us recharge and find mental clarity to any situation that may come our way.

Connecting to your breath means being present with it and feeling it move through your body with each inhalation and exhalation. As you do this, your mind and body naturally softens.

When feeling anxiety over a situation, go outside and breathe. Feeling stressed or nervous, go outside and breathe. Feeling overwhelmed, go outside and breathe. Need energy, go outside and breathe. Need a solution to a problem, go outside and breathe.

Go outside and breathe anytime to move stuck energy or simply to find quiet time.

While outside, look up and explore the vast open sky. Watch the clouds drifting by. Notice their shapes. Be curious about their movement. When a thought arises, allow the thought to become a cloud. Then let go of the cloud, watch it float away then rest your attention back in the sky and explore a little more.

- *Autumn retreats as a symbolic death, where some part of you must die before another part can emerge and come to life.*

- *Acceptance allows "what is" whether it is welcomed or not.*

- *Surrender is a willingness to trust life is working its way through you and everything will work out for your highest good.*

Nature is most seductive in the season of autumn as she performs her symbolic farewell dance of death and endings. Life, too, has its own season. The relationship died like the leaves in autumn, but the tree (you) still stands strong, and its (your) roots are still supported by the changing landscape.

When we reach the death experience of relationship endings, it's natural to crave rebirth. In the gap between endings and beginnings, we may not see what is in front of us on the road of uncertainty. However, up ahead is a new way to be free from the past when we allow life to take us where we need to go.

Acceptance is a stepping stone of letting go of attachments to the relationships and allowing what is. This is the path of least resistance we must travel to move one step closer to wholeness. Nothing in life is certain. Circumstances can change at any time. It's up to us to flow with the movement of our life.

Journey Notes

It was difficult leaving a long-term relationship but this was my fate. I didn't realize how deeply attached I was to the relationship, and losing my best friend of twenty-six years was hard. My heart was bursting with grief while my thoughts held me in a constant loop of reliving the past. To break free from the bondage I had to accept I was in uncharted territory. I had to acknowledge our journey together was over.

Holding onto illusions and fighting against the truth was my greatest struggle until I became honest with myself. I had to accept I was grieving a great loss of what I'd known for most of my adult life–being a couple. I had to accept there was no going back–divorce was the best possible solution for the both of us. I had to accept I was attached to a relationship that was not mine to hold onto–I was quickly replaced, he clearly had moved on.

Acceptance was the only way of walking onward to reclaim my life. When I did, there was an opportunity to *surrender* into my healing.

Surrender is a stepping stone of moving away from the things we have no power over. It becomes the path of least resistance in allowing life to manifest in divine timing.

Journey Notes

When I bowed before my challenges and just let my heart break, my life started to change. The healing journey was shifting in a new direction of forward movement–one stepping stone leads to another.

WINTER REGENERATION

JOURNEY INTO REFLECTION

"Look deep into nature, and then you will understand everything better."

Albert Einstein

On The Trail

HOUSE MOUNTAIN

Trailhead: House Mountain, TN
Features: Geological formations, cliff-top vistas
Rating: Moderate
Distance: 2-mile loop
Elevation: 1,000 ft.
Date: 12.05.09

Last night the weather reports predicted snow. I could barely sleep as my anticipation grew. After living in Florida for the last twenty years, visions of hiking in the snow danced in my head. The next morning, I was not disappointed as I quickly set out to House Mountain for my first snow hike.

The trailhead board mapped out several color-coded trails to navigate the way. A white trail led to the West End Overlook, a blue trail led to the East End Overlook and an inner trail intertwined with the two other trails that stretched across the crest of House Mountain. No getting lost as long as I followed the colored trail markers, but Father Winter had other plans.

With each step visibility diminished as the falling snow accumulated and the wind blew, making it difficult to see the trail markers attached to the trees. Doing my best to navigate through the blowing snow, I ended up taking a wrong turn here and there, leading to dead ends and backtracking to find the trail again.

After climbing two sets of fairly steep switchbacks, I finally made it to the ridgeline of House Mountain. The ground was untouched by footprints and an eerie hush fell across the forest.

Arriving at the overlook, I dusted the snow away and sat atop a large boulder. What was normally hidden by the trees during the growing season was now visible. Out in the distance the frozen landscape stretched for miles with picturesque views of the Smoky Mountains, as far as the eye could see.

Sitting there in the stillness of the forest, my thoughts enveloped me as a blanket of snow continued to gently fall. Frozen in time, ghosts of old hurts haunted me. I wondered if I'd ever find love again, or would I remain single forever. I didn't want to give up on love, but I was scared to death to give my heart away again. *Was I a failure at love?*

Sounds of flapping wings over my head snapped me out of my despair. The forest was stirring with sounds of movement. It was time to tackle the snowy trail again and start the slow descent down the mountain.

Back at the trailhead parking area, the snow had stopped and was melting away. On the drive back to the main road home, there was no real evidence it had snowed.

Glad I didn't miss this opportunity to explore hiking in the snow. I hope to get a chance to do it again someday.

Journey into Reflection

*Winter regeneration is a symbolic time
to explore and discover what is hidden
within the darkness for healing.*

AUTUMN GIVES WAY to a barren and stark setting as the landscape slowly lapses into a deep slumber. Light begins to fade away as the days grow shorter and the nights grows longer, triggering a period of dormancy during the darkest time of the year.

Under the lifeless winter landscape, what lies beneath the surface is where all the real work is taking place. Despite the overall empty appearance, transformation is always happening even if it's unseen.

Shifting into darkness is important for the overall health of Nature by forcing the environment into a state of rest. A time of regeneration before the next growing cycle can emerge renewed. This is her remedy, a part of her survival strategy meant to suspend the growing season.

Withdrawal and rest are vital to all living things. Sometimes it's wise to follow the instinct of Nature and withdraw for self-reflection.

Don't overlook the riches to be found in the darkness. There are tremendous insights waiting to be uncovered. Not all growth takes place in the light.

Then at the Winter Solstice, the longest night of the year reaches its fullness before returning to the expansion of light.

Inside the Alchemy of Winter

As the landscape slowly slips into regeneration, Nature compels us to turn inward, too. A time for a spiritual hibernation. A time to go on an archeological dig to explore our beliefs and feelings so healing can transpire.

This time of introspection and reflection offers a sanctuary to journey inside our inner world. Within the depths of our internal landscape, we become the excavators in uncovering who owns our identity and repressed feelings to release them into the light.

And if we come to treasure this time of darkness, we can explore inside our emotional center for self-reflection to understand ourselves a little more.

Letting go of who we have been and tapping into our emotional center is the alchemy of healing. There is much to discover as we land on the next two stepping stones of *Self-Identity* and *Feeling*.

Stepping Stone 4

SELF-IDENTITY

NOBODY PLANS FOR divorce when they get married. You fall in love and build a life together. When this life is shattered, it can leave you feeling like a failure or, worse, unlovable. Living in a society that holds the "until death do us part" belief and values being in a relationship for wholeness and completeness, challenges our healing.

We've been told by society what our roles are, particularly as women. These ideas have been instilled in our own belief system shaping our identity. However, if we dare to examine these roles, we will find they depend upon fitting into a conditioned society for security and approval.

We were born into a social order that values success where failure is frowned upon. The word "failure" is burdened with fear, shame and a whole lot of guilt. The truth is—there are no failures when life is happening for us, helping us to grow and evolve in this lifetime.

In life, circumstances change, people change and relationships change. Relationship endings are not personal failures, nor does it measure how worthy of love we are. And more importantly, our *self-identity* is not defined by being in a relationship.

Between endings and beginnings is a bridge that must be crossed to find what beliefs are encouraging forward movement and which are actually restrictive.

Who Owns Your Identity

It's possible you may have forgotten who you are, especially if you spent much of your relationship being the "right" person for your ex or identifying with your role as a spouse or a partner. It's easy to feel you've lost your sense of self after the breakup. You are not alone.

One of the deepest wounds of divorce and relationship endings is trying to understand who you are outside of a relationship on your own terms–not by society or familial terms.

We hear every day on the news, through television commercials, in magazines and on the internet how to fit in, how to look, how to be in this world. These messages become cultural spells that have been imposed upon us and can affect us at a deep core level, if we believe them to be true.

What we listen to and believe establishes a foundation of how we feel about ourselves and how we live our lives. Let's explore some of the cultural spells about divorce:

- Divorce is the easy way out.
- Divorce is a sign of failure.
- Divorce is a mark of shame.

These messages convey there is something wrong with us, and traps us in our own web of insecurities and fears. No matter what society says–your past does not define you. Don't allow the beliefs of others to determine your future.

It's never easy leaving a relationship; divorce can be healthier than staying in an unhealthy relationship. There are no personal failures, only experiences for growth. These shame-based thoughts compromises our way of being, which only influences how we show up in the world.

Identity is an obscure concept that leaves us buried under imposed beliefs as defined by our society and, worse, defined by our own self-imposed beliefs if we are craving for a connection to be accepted in society.

Divorce happens, relationships end, and how we identify with our beliefs is really up to us. We can believe our identity is attached to a failed marriage, or we can break through the cultural spells to gain self-mastery.

Exploration Journal

BELIEF SYSTEM

Being able to see yourself as a distinct, whole and separate person from what the relationship was restores a sense of purpose; rebuilding a connection back to who you are now becoming. Most often we live estranged from our true self because it's easy to look to the past and our external experiences as a way of defining who we are.

To uncover what beliefs you identify with, start by asking yourself:

1. Do I judge myself as a failure or unlovable?

2. Do I judge myself as unworthy of love?

If so, then consider the possibility that your identity is being self-controlled by the beliefs you hold. But whose beliefs are they? It's worth exploring more deeply.

By engaging in self-exploration, you're investigating what voice you are listening to that influences the way you live your life. This exercise will help to examine what beliefs are standing in your way, so you can claim freedom in moving ahead on the healing journey.

As you work with the prompts below, be willing to write whatever first impression enters into your awareness. Although you may be tempted to dismiss it, believe what you hear without over thinking it.

Start by placing your hand on your heart and being open to hear what is revealed.

3. How do I feel about being divorced?

4. Where did this belief come from?
5. Is this belief true for me?
6. How do I feel about being single?
7. Where did this belief come from?
8. Is this belief true for me?
9. Are my beliefs moving me forward or holding me back?
10. If I could be true to myself, without seeking approval or being afraid, what would that look and feel like?

You may not have chosen to end your relationship, but you do get to choose your beliefs about it in finding your *self-identity*. Realize you are not how society labels you. You don't need fixing to be accepted or to fit in. Nor are you the many things your former partner said about you in the relationship.

With a better understanding of your beliefs and where they stem from, you can start to change the internal self-talk that has been directing you.

Inner Coach Affirmation

MY PAST DOES NOT DEFINE ME

Thoughts are like drops of water. A drop becomes a puddle; a puddle becomes a pond; a pond becomes an ocean. If our thoughts are positive, we can float on the ocean of life. If our thoughts are negative, we can drown in the sea of life.

SELF-IDENTITY

I am
not
defined by
my past

Journey into Reflection

Stepping Stone 5

FEELING

WE LIVE IN a society that, in many ways, shuns emotional awareness. *Stiff upper lip; suck it up; grin and bear it; pull yourself up by your bootstraps; big girls/boys don't cry; emotions are a sign of weakness.* These messages have taught us not only to repress our feelings, but also to avoid them.

All too often we set our feelings aside, thinking they will go away in time. Avoiding unexpressed emotions only suppresses them, which gives them strength to grow while trying to conquer them into submission. Trying to force ourselves to feel a particular way does not support emotional awareness. It doesn't work and leaves us disconnected from our emotions that can lead to living in unhealthy ways.

Anytime we repress our feelings we are denying the truth of what is actually going on inside within us. When this happens, a force builds up that can lead to projecting our feelings onto others in harmful ways. Or, left unexplored, our feelings can fester into anger, resentment and depression. But, it doesn't have to be that way because contrary to what we've been taught, emotions are an essential part of being a human being.

Our soul longs for a rich connection with our emotions. *Feeling* is the alchemy of healing–leaving us more empowered to journey into wholeness.

We Are Emotional Beings

When our heartstrings are tied to those of another, we experience many feelings. For true healing to emerge it's important to build a relationship with our emotions. This relationship has the power to transform all areas of our life.

Our mind may be an expert at pushing away and denying feelings, but the body has no access to denial. The reality is; no matter how hard we might try to deny our feelings, they are always there. Emotions do not disappear. They stay in the body, seeking meaning before they can dissipate.

As a natural life force, emotions are intended to flow freely when we give them attention. When we allow ourselves to feel emotions rather than pushing them away, they will flow through us where we experience greater emotional well-being and freedom.

What lies buried within, is an opportunity to feel deeply into ourselves as the emotional beings we are for healing to transpire. When you feel—you heal!

When we experience our lives emotionally we begin to feel more connected to our inner world, which has the potential to carry us further along on the healing journey.

Feeling is Healing

When you love someone deeply and they are no longer in your life—let your heart break. It's messy; it's painful. But there is no detour around it. *Feeling* the heartache and all the emotions connected with it is the only way for true healing to take place.

A real after-effect of relationship endings are all the emotions we carry with us: sadness, fear, anger, guilt and shame. As we move through the healing journey our feelings can present a challenging aspect of our lives if left unexpressed.

Most times it's easier to believe that if we ignore our feelings then they'll just go away and then we unconsciously forget about them. The problem is–forgetting about them doesn't make them go away because emotions are a form of energy that ultimately becomes the emotional baggage we drag around with us when left unexpressed.

We can push unpleasant feelings away to avoid them, but eventually those feelings begin to pull on us. There's a saying: *what we resist–persists*, and it takes a lot of energy to contain stored emotional energy that will drain our vitality.

Inner Landscape

If you find yourself dwelling on all the things your former partner said or did to hurt you, or are being hard on yourself and *feeling* like you're responsible for everything that went wrong, it will be difficult to fully heal.

If you are seeking a new, loving relationship you will need to transmute those emotions as to not carry them into the next relationship. Making peace with your feelings not only builds a stronger foundation for a new relationship with another, it also creates a new foundation of living authentically with your own life.

All emotions are healthy, although at times it's challenging to work with them. The only requirement needed to honor our emotional well-being are acknowledgment and vulnerability. Acknowledging emotions to emerge is a way to validate them while vulnerability is a willingness to explore them.

Being vulnerable can be terrifying, but the places we don't want to go are the riches places to be. This process is similar to entering a chrysalis like a caterpillar preparing for a metamorphosis, before unfolding to break free. If the caterpillar feared the cocoon, it would never become the butterfly.

Exploration Journal

FEELING IS HEALING

By engaging directly with our emotions we have the ability to heal ourselves. When we spend time with them, they will travel freely through the body where a release happens and a *feeling* of peace comes showering down.

With this exercise, let's explore the inner landscape of your emotional realm to regenerate the natural flow of life for healing to transpire.

Before you begin have a box of tissues and a paper bag handy. It's possible to experience an emotional release. Tears are as natural as rain and if it happens you'll be prepared with no interruptions.

To begin, find a quiet place free from distractions. Take a deep breath and allow your body to relax as you drop your awareness down into the center of your belly. Feel into this sacred center and tell yourself; *it is safe to look within.* From this space of connection, wrap yourself with a sense of safety and love, suspending all self-judgments or criticisms.

1. Next, place your hand on your heart and ask yourself:

What am I *feeling* at this moment?

Listen for a response. Allow whatever enters your awareness without judgment.

2. After you identify the emotion, write down what you are *feeling:*

I feel (name it).

Sometimes just acknowledging an emotion and naming it, is enough to move it through the body. *Surrender* yourself to what is trying to flow through you. Then, sit for a few minutes by holding a loving space for the emotion to share with you any deeper insights.

> If you feel like crying, welcome it. Having a good cry moves the emotion and afterward, you'll feel better.

3. After the emotion has revealed itself, take a moment to let the words flow without editing them.

I feel (name the emotion) because . . .

Did you notice any tightness or unease? Sometimes a physical sensation is felt. When this happens you'll have to dig deeper, to find where the emotion is stored in the body before it can be fully expressed.

4. Next, direct your attention inward into your body. Take a moment to anchor into the center of your being (above the belly button area) by closing your eyes and taking a few deep breaths. With each exhalation, feel your body becoming more relaxed. Then ask yourself:

Where do I feel this emotion of anger (for example) in my body?

Notice where you feel the slightest bit of discomfort in your body, followed by an impulse to push away from the emotion. As best as you can, breathe into the area where you feel the most physical sensation. Resist criticizing or changing it. This only reinforces denial and begins a dialog that is not helpful. Flow with whatever presents itself.

5. As you move your attention into the body part where the emotion resides, allow yourself to completely experience it by asking:

What is this emotion trying to tell me?

Listen and allow the message to emerge. You may be surprised at what is revealed. A painful memory, an argument from the past, even an old childhood trauma could be triggered. Memories are powerful, and they can stay with you without even being fully aware you're still carrying them around.

> Once an emotion seeks meaning, it's not uncommon for the body to heat up as emotional energy flows through you. What's happening is a release of the built-up pressure from holding the emotion inside.

6. After the emotion has been felt, silently or out loud thank it for sharing its message. When you are ready, gently move your body around and finish by taking a nice, deep breath. Journal your experience; more insights may be revealed.

> After an emotional release, drink plenty of water. It's also helpful to take a warm soaking bath with Epsom salt (no longer than 20 minutes) to pull out any toxins the body may have built-up, followed by a shower to wash away any toxins remaining on the skin.

We release in layers. Deep feelings take time to clear. It may be helpful to check in with yourself daily by asking, "How am I *feeling* right now?" Each day will bring a new perspective. Whatever show up seeks meaning to move forward on the journey. Honor the process.

Inner Coach Affirmation

I HONOR MY EMOTIONS

It's been said that, "energy flows where energy goes." Meaning where you put your attention is where your energy is being directed. Your thoughts can weaken or strengthen your spirit. The energy it takes to engage with your thoughts is better served by shifting the inner dialog in another direction. Small actions have a powerful ripple effect.

FEELING

I
honor
my
emotions

Journey into Reflection

Alchemy Inside Nature

Have you noticed how a great sense of well-being falls around you when near an ocean, a lake, a waterfall, or even the rain? You feel relaxed and at peace with the world. That's because our bodies are being inundated by tens of thousands of negative ions created in Nature by the effects of water.

Scientists have found negative ions have a sedative, healing and pain-relieving effect, comparable to an anti-depressant prescription without taking a pill. Some people have also reported *feeling* better after a rainstorm when the air is highly charged with negative ions. This also explains how refreshing it feels to swim, take a shower or a bath.

The elemental energy of water makes us feel good by enhancing our mood, stimulating our senses, reducing anxiety, improving focus, and even helping us to sleep better.

Spend time near water to feel the cleansing effects it provides. Sit near water. Swim in a lake. Take a walk on a beach. Hike to a waterfall. Breathe in the energy and feel your energy shift.

Water is an essential element of life. We have a deep connection with water because we are mostly comprised of water. Spending time near, around and in bodies of water has the power to lift up our spirit to feel regenerated.

- *Winter regeneration is a symbolic time to explore and discover what is hidden within the darkness for healing.*

- *Between endings and beginnings is a bridge that must be crossed to find what beliefs are encouraging forward movement and which are actually restrictive.*

- *When we experience our lives emotionally we begin to feel more connected to our inner world that has the potential to carry us further along on the healing journey.*

In winter, we are reminded what lies beneath the lifeless surface is where all the real work is taking place. Transformation is always taking place through Nature's changing landscape, even if it is hidden in the hollow darkness. This is a sacred time of regeneration before the earth emerges renewed once gain.

Self-Identity is a stepping stone of understanding who owns our identity and how it affects the connection with our true self. In taking ownership of our belief system, not imposed by society, we are growing into wholeness. We are not defined by our society, our former partner, our history. They do not own our identity—unless we let them.

Journey Notes

My relationship was a part of my identity for nearly three decades. I didn't anticipate the identity crisis I would encounter. I felt like a complete failure. My beliefs led me to believe I was not capable of love as my thoughts cast a spell over me: *My marriage failed. There must be something wrong with me.* I was certainly walking the path of self-inflicted shame trying to fit into a society that values being in a relationship for wholeness.

I learned my identity is not defined by being in a relationship or by being divorced or by being single. It became quite clear I needed to live without shame or guilt if I was going to fully heal.

Feeling is a healing stepping stone of engaging directly with our emotions. Every emotion we have is telling us something. They become our faithful friends when we take the time to listen to them.

Emotions are an important part of the natural life force that is constantly moving through us. As we investigate our feelings, by giving them attention, we can offer care and support to clear any unresolved emotions that may otherwise stop the flow of life. If we have the courage to embrace our emotions, we awaken to an enormous expansion in moving forward on the healing journey.

Journey Notes

I thought I could just think my way through divorce; protect myself financially, protect myself materially and protect myself emotionally by avoiding my feelings.

Avoiding my feelings worked for me–until it didn't. When the wall cracked, every emotion I was *feeling* came crashing down like a tidal wave, knocking me to my knees and taking my breath away. Struggling to get away from them only made the waves stronger, pulling me down deeper until I surrendered and let the waves wash over me.

I learned emotions are like the weather, changing day to day: sometimes light, sometimes dark, at other times calm or intense. Resisting feelings is like trying to control the weather–it's impossible to dominate them.

SPRING RENEWAL

JOURNEY INTO TRANSFORMATION

"There is something infinitely healing in the repeated refrains of nature - the assurance that dawn comes after night, and spring after the winter."

Rachel Carson

On The Trail

LITTLE TRAIN WRECK

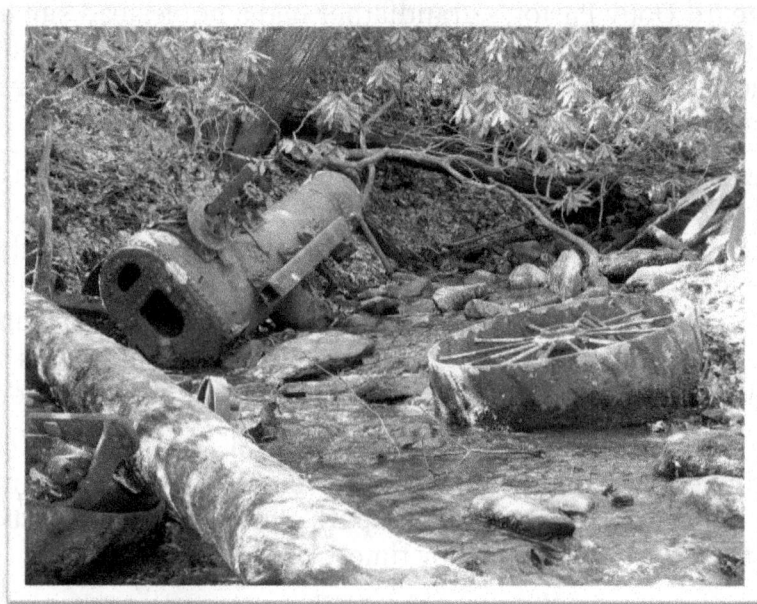

Trailhead: Grapeyard Ridge Trail, GSMNP
Features: History, Train Wreck
Rating: Moderate
Distance: 6.4 mile r/t
Elevation: 980 ft.
Date: 03.21.09

On the morning of the first day of spring, the temperature
was 34° but the sun was shining, gently warming the frozen

earth awake. It was a great day to explore where an old 1920's steam engine still rests at the bottom of Injun creek.

During the hike, it was clear spring had arrived. Daffodils and trilliums peeked through the ground. Mossy rocks shimmered in the sunlight. Canopies of rhododendron trees were starting to bud along the trail.

I heard Dolly Parton's grandfather had a homestead site in this area. No telling where. Remains of scattered stonewalls and old graves left impressions of mountain living of days gone by.

Grapeyard Trail rambled back and forth across Rhododendron Creek. Crossing the creek by rock hopping and log bridges provided amusement. Approaching the ridge of James Gap there was a patch of rhododendrons that offered a bird's eye view of the remains of an old steam engine resting in Injun Creek. I heard that Injun is a misspelling of "engine" most likely from an old mapmaker.

Storytellers say the driver lost control, and the engine tumbled down the hill into the creek. The old engine remains as a reminder of the park's history. A little rusty, yet relatively untouched by time.

After exploring the area, the trail continued another 1/4 mile to Campsite 32. A nice spot to stop for a snack and rest under large oak trees while staring into the deep blue sky before heading back down the trail.

Walking the trail from the opposite direction offered another viewpoint of the forest. Sometimes the trail didn't even look familiar.

While following the creek, a tree of interest caught my attention. Stopping for a closer inspection, I noticed how this tree had started as one from a seed and then it branched off as two separate trees with a shared trunk.

Although the trunk is now divided, it still shares a common connection that remains a part of both trees.

Studying it, there appeared to be a deeper meaning that I couldn't shake off. As the tree spoke to me, I heard its symbolic message.

This tree reminded me of my own relationship. Two people came together and planted the seed of love as one, growing together. When they stopping growing together, the relationship ended and they went their separate ways. Yet the connection of love still remains, this is their shared bond.

It occurred to me that love never dies; it just changes form. The love once shared will always remain in my heart. A-ha! That's where the love goes—it will always be a part of me.

Interesting how a new viewpoint welcomes a new perspective, in the least likely way.

Journey into Transformation

Spring brings renewal as a symbolic time of expansion through empowered actions.

THE EARTH GRADUALLY awakens from her dark slumber to embrace a new cycle of renewal. With the arrival of the Vernal Equinox, the once lifeless landscape changes form and starts to come alive. As the earth uncurls, movement gives way for the birthing of transformation.

New life emerges as the land pulsates with bustling activity. Spring rains give a nurturing drink to seedlings, beckoning tender new shoots of growth to break through the earth. Buds appear on naked branches of trees as the new growing cycle moves into rebirth.

At the heart of spring is the promise that life begins over, renewed after a time of regeneration. Moving deeper into healing, we can be liberated from the past by giving ourselves the nutrients we need to grow and expand.

Inside the Alchemy of Spring

In springtime, everything changes form and comes into being. Renewal encourages expansion as transformation takes place, similar to the emerging butterfly taking flight on untested wings.

A butterfly is one of the most inspiring symbols of transformation and rebirth. Before taking flight, it works through many stages before breaking free from the limitations of its cocoon in a new form. First, it will sacrifice

87

its old existence as a caterpillar before giving birth to the next level of transformation. Then the butterfly shape-shifts into being as a natural undertaking of its evolutionary growth. Not knowing whether it can fly, a butterfly unfolds to the process of expansion by taking flight as a new way of being in the world.

Transformation can be as natural as breathing when we trust our own unfolding into wholeness. Part of the transformational experience is an inner struggle before embracing the untapped potential within us that is waiting to be birthed.

Landing on the next two powerful stepping stones of *Self-Love* and *Forgiveness*, we discover a renewal of our own personal expansion as we *Journey into Transformation.*

Stepping Stone 6

SELF-LOVE

BEING IN LOVE with someone felt alive, and we felt good about ourselves. Now that the relationship has ended we may not feel so good about ourselves, leaving us to wonder if we'll ever experience love again. Sometimes this longing for love again leaves us seeking outside of ourselves to find the love we yearn for.

Often, after the ending of a relationship, we are left questioning if we are capable or worthy of love. Feeling unlovable is very real, and then we hold ourselves responsible for not being in love with another.

In struggling to find personal meaning, a typical reaction is to beat ourselves up about how imperfect we are. It's easy to believe the stories we tell ourselves. *I'm not good enough. There's something wrong with me.* This self-imposed thinking only creates feelings of disharmony, disconnecting us from healing completely.

No matter how messy your relationship ending was or how you feel about yourself at this moment, you are worthy of love because you exist. You are enough! No one else can make you feel anything less unless you let them.

Feeling whole again involves transforming your relationship with yourself. There is no escaping from the most important relationship in your life—the relationship you have with yourself! This will be a relationship that lasts a lifetime. Make it a loving one!

Transformation begins with being in the right relationship with yourself.

Cultivating Self-Love

Perhaps you've heard, "Learn to love yourself." Well, there's a good reason why—because it's easy to look for love in all the wrong places.

Love is not found outside yourself. Rather, the love you seek is inside of you waiting to be discovered. You were born innately with this love, and you've always had the power to access this for yourself. No one else can do this for you.

Self-love is an important seed thought to cultivate in having the right relationship with yourself. It's a declaration of self-worth and self-respect for the person you are. This doesn't come from someone else—it only comes from you! You are the love you seek.

By cultivating the seeds of *self-love*, you are planting a new thought process. These seeds, when watered and attended to, nourish your well-being that will bear the fruit of living in a way that supports and honors the person you are.

With loving attention, in time this new relationship encourages self-awareness and influences all aspects of your life. When you start loving yourself—your life will expand like a butterfly in flight. It starts with small steps.

Loving yourself is a practice that takes time. The more you attend to it, the more you will grow. Here are seven tips to sow the seeds of *self-love*.

SOWING SEEDS OF SELF-LOVE

1. Self-**Kindness**: An excellent first step is to treat yourself with kindness. The more you feel good about yourself, the more you will nurture your relationship with kindness. Each act of kindness, however, big or small, is watering the seeds of *self-love*. Start by doing something that makes you feel good daily by asking yourself; *What loving act of kindness can I do for myself today?* And then do it without over thinking it.

2. *Self-Care:* Put energy back into your life by taking care of your basic daily needs. Tend to proper nutrition, get enough sleep, walk or exercise. Paying attention and learning to understand what your needs are is a way to honor yourself on an ongoing basis. Be mindful of your choices by asking yourself; *does this choice honor me?* If the answer is "no" then simply don't do it.

3. *Self-Boundaries:* It's not helpful to go through the motions of doing what we *should* do for others because we are looking for approval from them. Set healthy boundaries that support your needs. Pay attention to activities that deplete you physically, emotionally and spiritually. Don't be afraid to know your limitations by asking yourself; *does this activity support me? Do I have time to do it without overextending myself?* If the answer is "no," then you are saying YES to you.

4. *Self-Awareness:* It's important to surround yourself with supportive people. Relationships are an exchange of energy. Be aware of which relationships are draining you. Take a moment to understand how a person makes you feel by asking yourself: *does this person support me?* If the answer is "no" then it's time to step back and put the relationship on hold. Sometimes people come into our lives to show us what we don't want or need. Don't spend time with people who are not supportive.

5. *Self-Compassion:* We can be compassionate when others reach out for our encouragement, yet all too often we fail to extend the same measure of compassion to ourselves. Don't be afraid to let people in who really care about you. If there is no one to turn to, then find a support group to help you through the challenges. You don't have to do it alone. Seeking help is not a sign of weakness, in fact, it supports well-being and is a loving act that you can extend to yourself.

6. *Self*-**Approval:** Develop your own appreciation. Believe you are capable of many things you may not even be aware of. Start to notice what's great about you and what you do well. Make a point of acknowledging your strengths and accomplishments on a regular basis. This practice will evoke self-worth and self-respect in your own capabilities as a person. As this happens, you become less attached to the opinions of others and more able to make decisions that support what you want and need.

7. *Self-Acceptance:* We live in an imperfect world. Nobody is meant to be perfect. Our own worst enemy is ourselves. It's easy to hear the harsh voice of the inner critic, but please don't engage in the conversation because it's not taking you where you need to be. Instead, weed out the thoughts by taking a moment to pause and telling yourself; *I am doing the best I can. I am not perfect. I am perfectly me.*

SELF-LOVE IN ACTION

Self-love is a healing ingredient that grows a loving relationship with yourself. Take action steps daily.

1. Begin your day with love: Greet yourself in a loving way by saying the words your spirit longs to hear. As you stand in front of a mirror, look deeply into your eyes and remind yourself you are loved by saying out loud, "I love and respect you, (state your name)." Repeat or even sing these words at least three times. If you are feeling resistance or are having a difficult time, simply try saying "I am willing to love you, (name)." Don't give up. Keep at it and in time the loving words will flow naturally.

2. *End your day with love:* Turn off the television, unplug from technology (including computer and cell phone) and allow yourself the simple luxury of doing something that is comforting for you. Read a book, take a bath, take a walk, sit outside, drink a cup of tea, a glass of wine, meditate, journal. This is your time to unwind and just be with yourself in quiet solitude. Enjoy it!

Growing Self-Love

A garden starts with laying down the soil then planting seeds, which are nurtured by the sun and watered with loving attention. At first, it appears nothing is happening, but with patience and tending the garden, plucking out weeds from time to time and fertilizing it, the garden will begin to grow and blossom.

Now consider how planting new seed thoughts of *self-love* will grow your relationship with yourself. Water the seeds with self-kindness and self-care. Set up self-boundaries and self-awareness to keep out intruders. Weed out any thoughts of doubt, fear and worry with self-compassion and self-approval. Fertilize it with thoughtful attention and self-acceptance.

One day your efforts will sprout and that loving relationship with yourself will blossom. If you quit tending to the little incremental actions that add up to a big difference, you'll miss the expansion of fully blossoming into who you are meant to be.

Exploration Journal

EXPANDING SELF-LOVE

The mind can be our harshest critic. It's wired for survival and questions everything we do. Although it's our mind's job to be the protector and look out for us, it can become the ultimate spell caster by telling us stories we begin to believe.

Over time those stories become difficult to ignore, which has the power to break down your inner spirit. Perhaps your inner critic self-talk sounds something like this:

- I'm not worthy. I'm not lovable. I'm a failure at love.
- I'll never find a loving relationship because I'm damaged goods, too old, not enough.

When we become attached to the stories it's easy to internalize those thoughts, making it difficult to love ourselves. These judgments become a way of life and then we accept them as part of who we are. Oftentimes we don't even realize just how self-critical we can become.

Once you become aware of self-imposed judgments, you can start building the right relationship with yourself.

First, let's discover how the inner critic shows up in your life.

1. List three ways you criticize yourself.

2. For each, describe why you criticize yourself.

3. How have these criticisms served you and others?

Next, let's uncover qualities you may have forgotten about yourself. Start by placing your hand on your heart and being open to hear what is revealed. As you ask yourself the below journal prompts, be willing to write whatever first impressions you receive. Although you may be tempted to dismiss them, believe what you hear and try not to over think it.

4. List three qualities (not physical attributes) you like and appreciate about yourself.

5. For each, describe how these qualities have served you and others.

> If you're having trouble writing this list, it means this process will benefit you the most if you keep working at it every day.

After completing your list, stand in front of a mirror and read the qualities you listed aloud to yourself. This process will open the flow of inspiration to love yourself a little more.

Finally, where in your life do you need to set up healthy boundaries for yourself?

6. What areas in your life are you tolerating and have avoided addressing?

7. Define three boundaries you can set up today.

> The next time someone asks you to do something, learn to say "maybe" and ask the person if you can get back with them after you check your schedule or after you think about it. This will allow you time to consider whether or not you can meet this commitment. It also allows you time to prepare and to get comfortable with how you will approach them. In time, you'll get used to the new you.

Inner Coach Affirmations

I LOVE AND RESPECT MYSELF

New seed thoughts of loving yourself will begin to take root in the days, weeks and months ahead. The smallest of actions can create the greatest transformation. It starts with the activation of your words through affirmations. They truly are the source of real transformation.

As you work with the affirmations below, it's best to either stand in front of a mirror or use a handheld mirror. When you look deeper beyond the self-image, you will see more than what appears in the reflection before you. The truth is—you are more than your body and your mind. Loving yourself is loving the true essence of your higher self, not your image or personality.

Start by looking into the mirror, gaze deeply into your eyes and say out loud the words your spirit longs to hear:

I love and respect you, (name).

I approve of you, (name).

Repeat at least twice more. Repetition activates the seed thoughts into being. Time and repetition are part of the process in sowing the seeds of *self-love.*

At first, you may feel uncomfortable when saying the words or become filled with emotions, especially if others or your former partner have berated your spirit for years. Please be patient and compassionate. And most importantly—don't give up on yourself. If you feel any resistance, try reciting:

I am willing to love and respect you, (name).

If you're still having trouble, then start with "*I am a friend to myself*" and gradually work from there. A small step at a time is perfectly fine. When the seed thoughts have taken root they will grow into a wonderful loving relationship with yourself.

Take a moment each morning before you start your day to give yourself a little loving.

SELF-LOVE

I love and respect myself

Journey into Transformation

Stepping Stone 7

Forgiveness

ALL RELATIONSHIPS BEGIN with the hope of a forever arrangement. There was a purpose and a time for being together. Although the time together is now over and you've gone your separate ways–was the relationship completed? Meaning, are there any unresolved hurts pulling you into the past to heal unfinished history alone?

Everything that fell apart and remains unfinished history is now waiting for completion. Without completion, we are left to remain forever connected to our former partner. And not in a healthy way.

Depending on how the relationship ended–bitter or sweet– it's common many people will not have an opportunity to complete their relationship ending in such a way of receiving full closure to put the past behind them. Most times the impact of divorce and relationship endings is much like a death that never ends.

Part of the relationship ending process can deny you the possibility of addressing hurts that happened in the relationship, which continue to affect you. These hurts echo in the present moment when triggered by some event and opens up an unhealed wound.

What triggers the past? Anything that takes you back to relive a situation, a conversation, a memory which still holds a strong emotional charge. Like a song playing on the radio where the words are so powerful they seem to reach down into the depth of our core. Triggers can happen at any time; they come up when least expected and when they do, they can leave you feeling the hurt a little more.

Old hurts can be transformed when we allow ourselves to openly practice *forgiveness* for true healing to happen. By choosing to forgive, we are choosing to complete our relationship ending regardless of what's happening with our former partner.

Liberation from old hurts begins with allowing forgiveness to set your heart free.

Completion

It's likely you will have interaction with your former partner whether it's co-parenting, living in the same town, or running into them with their new partner. It's how you relate to your former partner internally that will either keep you stuck in the past or moving forward in life. *Forgiveness* is how we heal our relationships with others to move into wholeness.

To complete the ending process from heartbreak into wholeness, we need to grant *forgiveness* to support our mental, physical and emotional health. We are human and nobody is perfect. Forgiving others for wrongdoings and forgiving ourselves for holding onto hurts is a way of understanding that we're all doing the best we can in an imperfect world. It's an important lesson to learn in any relationship.

If we are growing by our experiences, old hurts will wear our spirit down. We are not meant to carry heavy burdens of the past around with us. Every experience is an opportunity for growth and *forgiveness* is part of the experience as well.

Forgiveness will liberate you to be free from the past, by allowing old hurts to heal instead of feeding them with bitterness. Holding onto old hurts will not change the situation. For the most part, you will need to be in a place where the past no longer keeps you bonded together.

You may find it difficult to forgive your former spouse for unloving actions. It takes courage and a willingness to forgive someone who has caused pain. If you're willing to forgive them, that willingness feeds the possibilities of releasing hurtful memories.

Willingness

There is a saying: "Not forgiving is like drinking poison and expecting the other person to get hurt or die." Bitterness is the poison, and over time the only person it affects is you.

It's easy to hold onto all the hurtful memories of a relationship, stay anchored in the wounds of the past and have it define your life. When this happens, now the past becomes the future robbing you happiness from the life that is waiting to be embraced.

Some people never forgive. When this happens, they remain a victim by identifying with their hurts that will most likely impact future relationships and create a false sense of self-identity around the pain.

Forgiveness is forward movement on the healing journey. Otherwise, it's hard to move into wholeness and stay stuck in a long-lasting state of bitterness in your heart.

With *forgiveness*, you can let go of your own pain over wrongdoings. Once you get there, you are now ready to be liberated from the past and another person no longer controls your life.

Elixir of Life

Forgiveness is a healing remedy for life. It has the power to release an explosive energy of healing love to break the chains that bind us to another who has hurt or betrayed us.

Betrayal comes in many forms: a betrayal of trust, betrayal of actions, betrayal of support, any type of betrayal leaving us hurt. You can't change the past, but the past doesn't have to own you either. To forgive your former partner is the most effective treatment of healing from the pain that was caused.

But the truth is; it's easy to resist forgiving another because the voice of the false-self will scream, *"Why should I forgive him? Look at what he did to me! I'll never forget how he made me feel!" Forgiveness* breaks the power our mind wants to hold and liberates us to freely continue with a new life, rather than allowing our old life to intrude in the present.

Forgiveness brings wholeness if you choose to recognize your former partner as part of the journey in your life. If you do, you will heal the real pain. Understanding common myths about *forgiveness* will help break the spell of social conditioning.

5 FORGIVENESS MYTHS

Myth 1: *Forgiveness is a weakness.*

Truth: To forgive has the power to transform old hurts rather than being consumed by them. Did you know there is a center within you that is willing to release the hurt you are holding onto? This is the part of you that has the strength to navigate your life in the direction of freedom from painful experiences. *Forgiveness* is a sign of strength—it's a powerful gift you give to yourself.

Myth 2: *Forgiveness means agreeing with what happened.*

Truth: To forgive does not mean you approve or consent to what happened. Forgiveness will not change the past, but it will release the bond you're holding with another. Releasing this bond breaks the connection and when it happens; your former partner no longer holds power over your life. *Forgiveness* helps you to move further along on your path to wholeness.

Myth 3: *Forgiveness is not forgetting.*

Truth: To forgive is to let go and in time we do forget. As time marches on we do begin to forget the details, and how we felt fades away. When we do forgive we no longer hold onto old memories that would otherwise keep us stuck in a place remembering hurtful moments. *Forgiveness* opens a door to forgetting the pain.

Myth 4: *Forgiveness is about confronting another person.*

Truth: To forgive is a private experience with yourself and need not include the other person. It's not necessary to confront your former partner in any manner. The truth is; you may never get a resolution or an apology. Confrontation is not a solution, and it could possibly intensify a situation. *Forgiveness* is a loving act you can do for yourself to fully experience healing.

Myth 5: *Forgiveness benefits the other person.*

Truth: To forgive is about the relationship with yourself. Contrary to what many believe, *forgiveness* benefits you the most because it has the power to break a connection from another. It's an important step to take and is not conditional on whether your former partner takes part. *Forgiveness* is a personal liberation—it's meant for you and only you.

Self-Forgiveness

The act of *forgiveness* holds another, deeper purpose. At times, the person you need to also forgive is yourself because you cannot psychologically, emotionally, or mentally separate from the person who caused you pain. In turn, that pain is reflected back to you and now it's self-inflicted.

The pain of being hurt by someone else doesn't hold as much power as the pain caused by holding onto it. Keeping old hurts inside is how we cause greater pain to ourselves.

Ultimately, you will need to forgive yourself for holding onto those painful memories to restore wholeness. Self-*forgiveness* breaks down the wall of resentment and bitterness to heal the heart and to let love back in.

Forgiveness is a Destination

When true *forgiveness* transpires, the ripple effect spreads wide and far into our psyche making a huge difference in how we heal when another person has done us wrong. It unshackles us to enjoy life without any burdens. It's a destination helping us move further along on the healing journey into wholeness.

The decision to forgive is not an easy path to travel. Let's uncover the tools available so healing can continue to flourish.

Exploration Journal

FORGIVENESS RITE

One of the simplest ways to forgive your former partner is to write a letter telling them how they hurt you and how they made you feel. Let it out on paper and then burn it for complete liberation.

Find a quiet place where you won't be disturbed. Before getting started, take a few deep breaths and relax into the moment.

1. Begin by writing a list of the hurts that still have a hold on you by asking yourself; *what old hurts am I still holding onto?*

2. Next, tackle one item at a time from your list by writing a letter to your former partner. Write from the heart and allow yourself to say what needs to be said. Don't worry about editing yourself, since no one will read this letter. Allow yourself to express how you feel to fully convey what needs to be healed.

> The letter writing doesn't have to take place all at once. You may find it easier to undertake one item a day or one item a week. This is up to you. There is no right or wrong way.

It will take a lot of energy to do this exercise and may leave you feeling drained emotionally. If this happens, simply get up and start to move around by dancing, stretching or going for a walk. Any kind of movement will help release the energy.

3. After finishing the letter, fold it into thirds and write on it; "*I forgive you and set myself free.*"

4. The next step is important: don't leave the letter lying around in your home. It's best to take the letter outside and burn it. Find a safe place and container to burn the letter.

5. Begin by picturing the person in front you, light one end of the letter, then say out loud, "*I forgive you and set myself free.*" Place the letter in the container and let it burn. This signals an intention to manifest *forgiveness* out into the world.

6. After the letter is completely burned and the ashes have cooled off, dig a hole in the ground and bury the ashes. Or as an alternative, place them in a paper bag and immediately throw it out in the trash (not the trash inside your home).

Forgiveness is a gift we give to ourselves. Place your arms around yourself and give yourself a big hug. You have taken another powerful step towards wholeness.

Inner Coach Affirmations

I FORGIVE YOU AS I FORGIVE MYSELF

Affirm you are ready to set your spirit free and let go of the hurt from another person that is otherwise weighing down your spirit.

FORGIVENESS

I
forgive you
as I
forgive
myself

Journey into Transformation

Alchemy Inside Nature

FEEL THE EARTH

In a recent discovery, researchers have bridged the gap between an ancient tradition and modern times using science-based findings. Studies showed when the body is in direct contact with the earth, there is a grounding effect that changes our mood and improves our health. This time lapsed practice is now called, *earthing*.

The earth is a living organism pulsating with a natural healing resource promoting well-being. Although you may not necessarily see the earth's creative energy, you can actually feel it beneath your feet. All you have to do is walk barefoot on the earth to feel her vibration, to feel restored and grounded. How simple is that?

Since our feet have a rich network of nerve endings, walking barefoot is a simple, holistic treatment with abundant healing qualities. When we connect the soles of our feet to the earth's surface our bodies absorb the vibrational energy field of electrons, which provides needed negative ions to help restore balance.

When feeling stressed, anxious, foggy, depressed, or out of balance, all you have to do is find a natural environment, take off your shoes and socks and expose yourself to the renewable flow of healing our Earth Mother naturally provides.

Sink your feet into the earth to feel the movement of her primordial energy restoring and recharging your mind, body and spirit. Walk as if you are kissing the earth with your feet. If you feel a tingling sensation or a warmth rising up from your feet, don't worry–that's just the earth re-energizing your body as she kisses you back.

Remember, the same creative energy that makes up the living earth is also a part of you. Make a connection by touching the very earth you live on, to receive her healing powers by *earthing*.

ALCHEMY OF HEALING

- *Spring brings renewal as a symbolic time of expansion through empowered actions.*

- *Transformation begins with being in the right relationship with yourself.*

- *Liberation from old hurts begins with allowing forgiveness to set your heart free.*

The promise of Nature is that she never breaks her growing cycle. She will always bring life back to the landscape once again after a time of regeneration. We don't have to wonder what season comes next as the pattern of movement flows into rebirth.

Drawing upon the alchemy of spring, we can transform the relationship with ourselves after a time of reflection as renewal comes alive.

Self-Love is a stepping stone of planting new seed thoughts to reawaken a loving connection with yourself that will stand the test of time.

Words have creative power, every thought we think is a seed. These seeds, like the seeds of a flower, will sprout under the right conditions when extending self-care to yourself. By cultivating a loving relationship with yourself, you can transform the flow of your life.

Journey Notes

When I planted the seeds of *self-love*, I stopped blaming myself for everything that went wrong in my marriage. I felt unlovable and felt unworthy of having a meaningful relationship again. As I nurtured a loving relationship with myself, I realized we had both played roles and stopped pointing the finger at myself. My self-worth was restored.

Affirming, "I love and accept you, Laura" was a great transformational tool that had a major impact on how I felt about myself. For the first time in my life, I understood giving myself permission to be my authentic self, starts with self-approval towards the person I am. Life is not perfect and neither am I. By embracing all aspects of myself, I was building a solid connection with the one person who will always be in my life—me. This is a relationship to cherish.

~~~⁂~~~

Forgiveness is a stepping stone with the greatest potential in transforming hurtful experiences and bringing a completion to any relationship ending.

Journey Notes

Most of the time I found myself thinking about and going over the same stories of what happened, how it happened and how it felt. These old stories haunted me. Every time I was triggered by the past I was stuck in a time warp, feeding the hurt a little more.

I learned practicing *forgiveness* was the only way to release the old stories that were revisiting me. Now when I get hooked I can easily say, "I forgive you as I forgive myself" and the ghost of the past fades away. It sounds too easy, right? In my experience, those words are a great source of power in helping me to move forward on the journey of life.

~~~⁂~~~

SUMMER RECOVERY

JOURNEY INTO INTEGRATION

"Earth laughs in flowers."
Ralph Waldo Emerson

On The Trail

RAMSEY CASCADES

Trailhead: Ramsey Cascades Trail, GSMNP
Features: Log bridges, waterfall
Rating: Difficult
Distance: 8-mile r/t
Elevation: 2,140 ft.
Date: 8.8.2009

Surrounded by a beautiful setting made this eight-mile roundtrip hike to the largest waterfall in the Great Smoky Mountains National Park worth every step.

Driving the bumpy road to the trailhead parallels the Little Pigeon River. With parking areas to pull off, there are large rocks to sit on and take in the natural beauty. Note to self: learn to fly fish.

Most of the hike was a gradual uphill incline that followed the Middle Prong stream. Listening to the sounds of water in the background was hypnotizing and helping me to forget just how long this hike really was.

Crossing the stream on log footbridges was part of the adventure on this trail, making it memorable. There was much to explore in the ever-changing landscape of this magical walk in the woods.

Around the halfway mark a rock staircase appeared, turned a corner, and faded away into the forest. Following the stairs, one stepping stone at a time, led into a green canopy of rhododendron trees.

Carefully watching each step, the gnarly tree roots demanded sure footing over the earth's rocky terrain. Another enchanting feature of this rigorous trail.

Approaching the last two miles, the trail passed through one of the largest remaining old-growth forests in the Smoky Mountains. Within the grove, a giant tree with a trunk over eight feet in diameter caught my attention. Standing at the base of this towering tree, I had to hug it. Wow! I could feel love emanating deep from its roots into her nurturing fullness. What a feeling of connection with the forest.

The last stretch was the most challenging part of the hike, as the rocky trail started a steep climb to reach its final destination. For good measure, a few switchbacks tested my true commitment. Hearing the rushing water was the motivation to keep going. The waterfall was close. There was no turning back!

With each step the music of rushing water was increasingly getting louder, cheering me on to continue. Moving closer, an opening appeared revealing a hint of the waterfall that awaited. Just a few more feet to go. Wait for it! Almost there! And then—there it stood in all its glory. It literally took my breath away!

To get a closer look, I took off my boots and socks and carefully lowered myself over large boulders to explore the waterfall. After walking four miles, my feet were ready to enjoy a cool drink of refreshment.

Ramsey Cascades is one of the most impressive waterfalls in the Smokies. It stands roughly 90 feet high with a cascading water run of 100 feet emptying into a small pond. There's an unmarked path leading down to the pond that requires maneuvering over slippery rocks.

Experiencing and appreciating the beauty of this strenuous eight-mile trail was worth every step. In fact, I went back again, and hopefully I'll hike it again another day.

Journey into Integration

*Summer arrives as a symbolic time of
growth to integrate the return of wholeness.*

SEEDS SOWN IN springtime have taken root and are blossoming with a great depth of richness. Growth of lushness spreads across the landscape, maturing into fullness as the sun and the earth unite to feed the fertility of the land into wholeness.

Gradually the intensity of sunlight grows brighter. At the Summer Solstice the sun will reach its highest peak, marking the longest day of the year. Then, slowly, the earth will turn towards the end of another growing season to yield her fruit.

Everything in Nature is integrated and interrelated. There's an organic progression of movement activating new growth, paving the way with a restored sense of being alive.

This movement of growth engages new possibilities every day, creating a natural flow with life as the natural world celebrates each day with the arrival of a new dawn.

Inside the Alchemy of Summer

If only for a moment, time stands still as we gaze upon the sun breaking over the horizon each morning, and then dipping under the horizon to settle in each night. Nature doesn't disappoint, for the sun will rise again with the promise of a new day that only tomorrow brings.

A sunrise urges us to move ahead, not to dwell in the past and to begin where we are now. The birth of a new day is a compelling symbol of hope and possibilities. It holds the vow of ushering in a new beginning with a new opportunity to start refreshed.

At a deeper level, summertime welcomes new growth calling forth a horizon of possibilities. A time to shine our light and to ignite our dreams on the next exciting destination of our journey called life.

Through the movement of healing, one stepping stone at a time, the worst weather is behind you. You are now in the flow of your own growth and potential. A time to integrate all that has been experienced, and to envision new possibilities.

Honoring where you have been, you can now appreciate the journey from heartbreak to the return of wholeness as a rite of passage. A celebration to harvest the fruits of fertility and the abundance of all the changes that have taken place while on the healing journey.

The inner work is completed, and every stepping stone has deepened your connection back to yourself.

Now it's time to fully embody the healing received and to begin your own independent journey into *co-creating* an inspired life. How do you do this?

By landing onto the last two stepping stones of *Gratitude* and *Co-Creation*, as we *Journey into Integration*.

Stepping Stone 8

GRATITUDE

RELATIONSHIPS ARE NOT by accident. People are put together for a reason—to experience a union. Sometimes our journey together with another involves pain that cannot be explained.

After the ending of the relationship, a meaningful purpose flourishes in unseen ways that could not otherwise possibly happen if we had stayed together with that person.

Every relationship with another person paves the way for a new journey of experiences to explore. And it's important to be able to harvest those experiences through *gratitude*. It's a process that gives depth to the relationship through what has been learned about ourselves through another.

When the healing journey began, it was a time that felt like everything was crumbling. Left standing at a crossroads, you may have found it difficult to see the forest for the trees. Walking one step at a time into the unknown was the only way out.

Now, where you are standing, you can find something to be grateful about. You can choose to see the blessings within the challenges faced along the way, helping to give meaning to all that has been experienced.

You now see the world and yourself through a new lens of awareness that paves the way with a rekindled sense of renewed possibility of what lies ahead.

Gratitude opens a gateway to living in the present moment.

Cultivating Gratitude

Understanding how far you have traveled on the healing journey is acknowledging how much you have grown. You are not the same person as when you started the journey, in part because of moving through self-exploration and doing the inner work to rise strongly out of the pain of a heartbreak.

Take a few moments right now to just breathe and be thankful for being alive. Feel the love and compassion *gratitude* brings into your heart.

Gratitude is a way of returning to grace and grows your presence within it. It's an invitation to notice the world around you and how it impacts your life. Life reveals grace in every waking moment when we take the time to notice.

There is always something to notice about life that encourages an attitude of *gratitude* to its fullest expression of appreciation. The deeper you appreciate, the more your life flows in harmony with the creative current where life is happening for you.

Consider all the things in your life you could be thankful for: your home for providing shelter, your car for providing transportation, your food for providing nourishment to your body, your job for providing financial support, your friends and family for their emotional support, your pets for their unconditional love, your special items that comfort you, and the list goes on.

One way to cultivate *gratitude* is by making a daily commitment to intentionally reflect upon your day. As you do, you develop a valuable practice of paying attention to the people, places and activities present in your life.

4 GRATITUDE TIPS

A *gratitude* practice creates a new flow of energy changing the way you observe life. Creating a practice of being thankful every day, especially for the little things, will expand your life in many ways. Try it and notice how you feel. Here are a few ways to help connect you with *gratitude*:

1. ***Take Notice***: What did you notice today? Think about the most beautiful thing you saw today and how it made you feel. If you can't think of anything, go outside. Look around and recite what you see with grace. "I'm grateful for the warmth of the sun. I'm grateful for this beautiful view." Start outside and work your way inside your home, naming everything that makes you feel good. Notice new things every day.

2. ***Inspiration***: What or who inspired you today? A song, a painting, a quote, a book, watching a sunset. How about the people in your life that inspire you? Think of one specific thing about each of those people that brings *gratitude* for being in your life.

3. ***Celebrate the Wins***: Identify three good things that happened today. They can be big like "I am grateful for my promotion" or as simple as "I am grateful I found time to walk in the park" or as profound as "I am grateful that I realized I was not my best self today and tomorrow is a new day."

4. ***Review Your Day***: Before falling asleep, take a moment to review your day and name at least five things you are thankful for. It's a great way to cultivate all of your experiences. If you find yourself lying awake with worry, this practice can shift your thoughts to help sleep come more easily.

Exploration Journal

HARVESTING GRATITUDE

Real transformation has taken place through the healing process. Everything you needed to know about yourself was uncovered on the healing journey, and now it's time to harvest the growth of your experience.

Let's discover how far you've traveled where new insights play out with a new awareness. In this journal exercise, it's important to embrace the healing experience with honesty. Take your time as you answer each prompt below.

1. What were the toughest challenges you had to overcome before embarking on a journey into healing?

2. List the biggest changes you experienced on this healing journey.

3. What strengths did you develop during this transition that you are most grateful for?

4. Describe how you changed your beliefs around divorce, breakups and being single.

5. What did you learn about yourself that you didn't know when the journey started?

By harvesting the healing experience you can make *gratitude* a part of our personal story of turning heartbreak into wholeness.

Inner Coach Affirmation

I AM GRATEFUL FOR ALL EXPERIENCES

Gratitude grows a powerful connection to every experience as life presents itself to you and through you. By reflecting on each day, you create a profound sense of sacredness and richness with your life.

GRATITUDE

I am grateful for all experiences

Journey into Integration

Stepping Stone 9

CO-CREATION

IN ANCIENT TIMES alchemy was shrouded in magic and mystery. The alchemist's purpose was inspired by a desire to transform some form of matter (lead) into another expression of itself (gold). This desire invokes the *co-creation* possibility of manifesting inspiration into a life full of potential with endless possibilities.

Driven by inspiration, we are all alchemists. Every person either consciously or unconsciously uses the alchemist's power of *co-creation*. How? It starts with an idea or inspiration as simple as, "I want a new job." Then, by thinking about it, imagining it, and taking action steps, inspiration manifests to fruition.

A thought motivates any intention, which then guides the energy *co-creation* to flow into form that expresses into reality.

Within everyone resides the alchemist. We are all *co-creators* by design. What a powerful thought. You are more powerful than you know. You not only have the power to manifest what you desire—you are the power. You always had it.

Every person is destined to live an inspired life. Choosing to be led by our deepest desires of creative expression is the motivation in achieving all that is possible. All we have to do is follow our heart and feel the magic to actively take part in the process of *co-creating* the life we desire.

Designing the life you want is a creative process.

Self-Trust

Moving from heartbreak into wholeness, for some, the pathway is clear as to the next steps that will bring the most satisfaction and happiness. Perhaps it's finding a new relationship, a new home or a new career. Perhaps it's financial security or more prosperity. Perhaps it's more adventure or joy.

Any time you step into creating a greater version of life, there comes a new need to believe and trust in yourself a little more. The person you need to believe in the most is *yourself*. Self-trust is the currency of your spirit. It encourages you to pursue your dreams without limitation.

Activating self-trust to pursue your inspirations will determine the next step paving a direct route to fulfilling what is possible for you to live in alignment with your desires.

It's easy to be pulled into fear and doubt that obstructs your ability to go after your dreams. Fear can stop you dead in your tracks when you don't know how or when it can be achieved. Nothing is really in your way. It's only the lack of self-trust stopping you from believing that everything will work out in creating the inspired life you want to live.

It's important to trust yourself because only *you* know what's best for you. No one gets to live your life unless you give your power away to them. You get to choose your dreams. Only you can determine how life looks for you.

Your dreams want to be lived through you. When you're willing to listen to your heart and take action, then one step often leads to the next step that will always be right in front of you. This is how the alchemy of *co-creation* begins.

Inner Compass

Often when deciding to do something, we allow our rational minds to navigate the way. We tend to rely on it to guide us, yet the real danger is believing this is real guidance.

You see, the mind will influence us with one of the biggest lies: *Who do you think you are to dream so big?* The truth is, the heart taps into pure knowledge and is far more accurate than our minds.

When you pay attention to your heart, your inner compass, you will always be guided on the right path to achieve your dreams. Your heart's desire will always guide you.

Have you ever felt a warmth in your heart when something felt right? That's a guidepost, a beacon of light, to follow what feels right for you. Sadly, the mind does not offer the same encouragement.

When you actively choose to be led by your heart, you open the field of possibilities to finding happiness and satisfaction meant for you to experience. You have the power to *co-create* anything you want in your life and design the life you want to live.

If you believe, then the question of creating your best life becomes, "What would I do if I wasn't afraid?" By asking yourself this powerful question, a nugget of gold is revealed activating a magnetic energy of flow in living the inspired life that is meant especially for you.

Inspired Living

Every single person in this world needs to walk his or her own path. Sometimes we follow a path that has been paved by others when we are left to compromise our dreams.

Your life is unique and nobody else in this world can tell you what's best for you. Don't let your fears get in the way of your heart's desire. Don't let other people's opinions hold you back from living an inspired life. And don't be afraid to forge your own path, even if that means you have to move beyond your comfort zone.

Having a clear understanding of what you would like to experience more in your life begins the process.

By now, you most likely know what you don't want in your life. Now is the time to point your life in the direction of what you do want. Once you get clear on what it is and take inspired action, you will notice that life will flow in the direction of you where you want to go.

Exploration Journal

A New Vision

The first step in *co-creation* is connecting with the right desire. Many of us have fallen into the trap of being guided by our false-selves rather than our hearts.

1. Ask the Heart

First, place your hand on your heart and breathe down into the center of your belly to the place where your creative energy is stored. Then write in your journal any or all of the following prompts:

- What inspires me at this moment?
- What do I desire to create in my life right now?
- What am I curious about to explore?

Then be still and listen for the answer. It will be the first impression you receive. Acknowledge what shows up and quickly write it down in your journal before you second guess yourself.

> Working through this exercise takes time. If you're having difficulty, find clarity by going outside or taking a walk. Sometimes the answer will come when you are completely relaxed. An inspiration or an idea can enter your awareness at any given time. Be open to receive it.

2. Explore the Desire

Next, dig a little deeper to determine if this is a desire you believe in. Sometimes we pursue a desire we think we want but it turns out we aren't willing to commit to it wholeheartedly. Ask yourself:

Do I believe (name the desire) can be achieved?

Write the first word that comes to mind and feel any sensation. Be willing to move on to another desire by repeating the above process again. Remember to listen from the heart, not the head. When you believe in the right desire, you are more invested in achieving it.

> A feeling of hesitation can indicate your desire or goal is not meant for you. It could also mean the timing isn't right yet, and the desire needs more time to incubate.

3. Test the Desire

Testing the desire is the quickest way to feel if it belongs to you. Start again by placing your hand on your heart, taking a breath into the center of your belly and then asking yourself:

Will (name the desire) make me happy?

Notice any emotion you feel while writing the answer. Happiness, excitement or joy is a good sign. If fear or doubt is aroused, that's a sign something big is happening and it's all the more reason to pursue it. This happens when you dare to dream big.

4. Take Action Steps

Action steps are necessary to support the flow of movement. When a sign presents itself, it's up to us to light the spark to lead the way.

For instance, you may feel a strong impulse to buy a certain book, attend a workshop, take a trip somewhere, or call a friend. Don't discount what appears to be out of the norm. This is how the *co-creation* sparks works. Trust the process.

5. Attitude of *Gratitude*

The more you stay in *gratitude*, the stronger your connection grows to manifest that which is unseen into your reality. Realize there is also a possibility something even better than your original desire will come to you.

Trust you're being led down a path as one step leads to another, and then it all falls into place. The more you open yourself to life, the more you will receive. The end result will happen as long as you keep things moving. Be patient and enjoy the process as you allow an inspired life to live through you.

Inner Coach Affirmation

I AM THE CO-CREATOR OF MY LIFE

Every thought we think is an affirmation. Our thoughts have their own magnetic energy that manifests into form. We always attract into our lives what we think about the most. Each thought shapes the life we choose to lead.

CO-CREATION

I am
the
co-creator
of my life

Journey into Integration

Alchemy Inside Nature

FIRE IN THE SKY

When was the last time you stopped to watch the rising or setting sun long enough for it to fill your heart with hope?

The promise of a new day always emerges as the sun rises from under the covers of the land, announcing good morning to all. Glowing brighter as it rises higher in the sky to shine its guiding light upon us. Even on a cloudy day, after the parting of the clouds, the sun will always be shining. The sun will never fail to shine; this we can rely on.

Throughout the day, the sun will gradually travel across the sky as it slowly creeps back under the horizon. Before casting a blanket of darkness, the sky is set on fire with a crescendo of colors as a goodnight kiss to all marking the end of another day.

Then without fail, the sun will rise once again bringing a new day of hope. It will never let us down; it will always dawn a new day, encouraging us to live in a new way.

Sunrises and sunsets are Nature's fleeting creations. No two are alike. They have the power to take our breath away like love.

Life has a way of taking over, leaving the simple pleasures behind to be left unexperienced Make time to enjoy the natural beauty of a sunrise or sunset more often to stay connected to the promise of a new day.

Savor every moment of that fleeting beauty. They are true awe-inspiring wonders to behold.

ALCHEMY OF HEALING

- *Summer arrives as a symbolic time of growth to integrate the return of wholeness.*

- *Gratitude opens a gateway to living in the present moment.*

- *Designing the life you want is a creative process.*

Looking at where you've been to see how far you've traveled now becomes your personal integrative journey of healing from heartbreak. When you can look back into your past with no regrets, you embrace the fullness of life to consciously harvest each experience. It's not where you've been, but where you are going that is to be celebrated.

Gratitude is a stepping stone that activates awareness, and a connection to welcome everything into our lives. The smallest, tiniest, minute moments in our days provide a mindful view of grace. There is always something to be thankful for when we take the time to notice.

Journey Notes

I learned so much about myself after the ending of my marriage. Moving to a new state, I learned to trust myself. I found new ways to generate income by pursuing what I love. I had forgotten how much I enjoyed the four seasons. Hiking and exploring revived the missing parts of myself that were put away for far too long. I learned to love myself. The growth I experienced couldn't have happened any other way. There was so much to be grateful for.

136

Co-Creation is a stepping stone that has the potential to inspire a creative life. All your dreams already exist and are just waiting for you to wield your own magic to make them happen.

Journey Notes

After all the legal matters were settled, I knew I would be leaving my marital home to rebuild my life, although I didn't know where. I knew something was waiting for me. Then one day I placed my hand on my heart and asked for guidance.

Later that day I heard *"go to Tennessee,"* whispered as an inspiration. Although my mind had some resistance, in the end I had nothing to lose by moving there. When I arrived in Knoxville it felt like home, and I instantly knew I belonged there. Following the direction of my inner compass was the best thing I ever did. This is where my healing journey took place giving me the courage to experience life with more awareness.

Full Circle

Healing doesn't mean heartbreak never existed.
Healing means a return to wholeness to love again.

WE ARE ON a sacred journey of change, discovery, transformation and movement. The path in front of us brings challenges and triumphs that speak to us every step of the way. How we navigate the twists and turns will have a huge impact on how we approach life.

Divorce and relationship endings have the power to transform the lives of those who are fated to go through it. There's no denying–it takes a personal commitment and courage to walk the healing path back to wholeness.

From heartbreak into wholeness, you are now invited to flow in the river of life with an understanding that life is happening for you and not to you, encouraging new experiences to explore and new ways to be. Going with the flow means to be open and to trust the process of life that will carry you where you need to go for growth.

Movement of Life

Life will always ebb and flow; moving us through unexpected change. There will be uncertainty along the way, since we can't plan how life will happen *for* us.

We are all on a spiritual path whether we acknowledge it or not. Our purpose is to grow and evolve. Life will present opportunities for growth within each experience presented on our journey. Sometimes they will lift us up with joy and other times knock us to our knees with sorrow.

This life is meant especially for you to explore. At times it can be overwhelming not knowing the way, but it's important to remember that life is an active process of movement with many destinations to experience. Embracing the movement of life encourages us to explore life a little more.

Parting Ways

As you move forward in life be aware of what might trigger an old hurt that still resides within. Since you have a historic relationship with your former partner, echoes of the past may creep in seeking attention. Sometimes it may feel like you're taking two steps back, but healing can be an ongoing process. Know you are not regressing and use the tools outlined here to clear the path ahead once again.

Spend more time in Nature to connect back to yourself. Look up into the sky every day and notice the natural world that surrounds you.

Never stop learning who you are. Continue a path of self-discovery. Every experience is yours to explore. You may be surprised what you discover about yourself along the way.

For every ending there is a new beginning—you are now stepping onto the path of a wonderful new journey!

You are now open to love freely again!

Reflective Thoughts

*The lover of nature is he whose inward and outward
senses are still truly adjusted to each other.*
Ralph Emerson Waldo

I WOULD HAVE never imagined I would be divorced. We loved each other and even though we tried to make our marriage work, in the end, our love story ended. And when it ended, I never would have imagined the vulnerability and pain I would feel leaving me broken wide open. There was nothing left but to rebuild my life.

This meant walking into the unknown to face all the emotions I was feeling and finding answers as to why I had to experience this kind of heartbreak. It was also an incredible soul-searching journey in which I learned so much and grew in ways I could never have imagined.

Looking back at my healing journey, I realized most obstacles in life are spiritual ones. Understanding that life was happening for me became an anchor helping me to follow the signs in forging a path to wholeness. Although the signs were unclear at times, and I felt lost at other times, it required a leap of faith to get where I needed to go.

One of the things I've learned about life is we don't always have control over our circumstances. Sometimes life is beautiful, sometimes life is messy. No matter what happens there is a great force always guiding us. Life will always meet us where we are. It's up to us to say "yes" to whatever is presented along the way.

I learned love is the most powerful emotion we can feel. Love can lift us up and love can take us down like a crushing force that can break us. When love turns into heartache, it becomes one of our greatest spiritual teachers of all—it means you had the courage to love another. Letting your heart break leads to a path of healing where you can love freely again.

One day I stopped thinking about the past; stopped thinking about everything that went wrong; stopped thinking about my former partner. One day I no longer felt heartache and life was moving in a new direction, leaving behind a dusty trail.

What lies on the path ahead are more experiences to explore with a new awareness that life is happening for me and not to me.

The more time I spent in Nature, the more I experienced her energetic creative alchemy. With every breath, I was being restored to wholeness. Within her nurturing arms, I intuitively understood her language also speaks to the human condition of navigating through life. This is the greatest gift I received. I hold it dearly.

The Smoky Mountains hold a personal meaning for me. I learned they are among the oldest mountains in the world, dating back 200 to 300 million years ago. This ancient mountain range holds a magical allure that captivated my spirit. Exploring these mountains filled my heart with a knowing that this was where I needed to be during a painful time in my life.

What I learned from heartbreak and suffering has led to a meaningful connection with life. Although my relationship ending was painful, it had a purpose and became a profound experience.

I did my inner work. I put the shattered pieces of myself back together one stepping stone at a time. Now I can wholeheartedly say; *I am open to love freely!*

⚬✕⚬

In Gratitude

This book was birthed during my journey of healing while living in Knoxville, TN, and hiking in the Great Smoky Mountains National Park. Every person I met on this journey had an impact in my life. I will always be grateful for the wonderful memories and friendships made along the way.

Thank you Steve for being a part of my life—you were one of my greatest teachers. My love for you will never die, and I hold a special place for you in my heart. The ending of our relationship led me to embark on a journey that was not only healing; it also turned into my work to share with others.

Thank you Ed for your unconditional friendship. You held the space for me during this difficult time. I am grateful our paths crossed.

Thanks to my editor Karren Tolliver, who put me to task and also became part of this journey.

Special gratitude to my mother (who transitioned during the writing of this book. I know you are smiling down upon me.), my dad and my sister, Jasmine, for their love and support.

About Laura Annan

Life is a journey...happening for us...enjoy every mile!

As a licensed Heal Your Life® Teacher and certified meditation and yoga instructor, Laura Annan has over 15 years of experience in personal development and holistic healing modalities. After the ending of her 25-year marriage, she moved to the mountains seeking a new beginning. This transformational inner journey inspired Laura to translate her personal experience of healing into nine stepping stones to navigate the way from heartbreak into wholeness.

Other books by Laura Annan include <u>Healing by Nature: Reflections of the Heart</u> and <u>Stepping Stones to Heal Endings,</u> a five-eBook series. Her essay *"Dancing with the Leaves of Change"* was published in the <u>Fall: Women's Stories and Poems for the Season of Wisdom and Gratitude</u> anthology. She also writes for various publications.

With a desire to explore, on any given day Laura can be found walking in Nature, finding serenity and capturing moments with her camera.

A Note from the Author

Thank you for reading my book!

I'd love your feedback. Would you please consider rating and reviewing this book? Thank you!

www.ingramcontent.com/pod-product-compliance
Lightning Source LLC
Chambersburg PA
CBHW061726020426
42331CB00006B/1110